Scots and Scotch Irish

Scots and Scotch Irish

Frontier Life in North Carolina, Virginia, and Kentucky

Larry J. Hoefling

INLANDIA

SCOTS AND SCOTCH IRISH: FRONTIER LIFE IN NORTH CAROLINA, VIRGINIA, AND KENTUCKY is a publication of Inlandia Press, portions of this work previously appeared under the title Chasing the Frontier, iUniverse, 2005.

INLANDIA press
b. a. oklahoma

ISBN 978-0-9822313-2-6

First Trade Printing: June 2009

Manufactured in the United States of America.
http://inlandiapress.com

For Kristen and Ronnie

And the Beginnings of their own Legacy

CHAPTER ONE

Before the Crossing

In the lowlands of Scotland, in the rugged and desperate country of the early seventeenth century, there lived a sturdy race of Gaelic heritage whose civil isolationism left them dramatically entrenched in conditions that would easily pass for the Middle Ages. In fact, Scotland was undergoing a change, emerging ideas and progressive attitudes hinted that the country might be dragged out of the dark into the light of civilization.

They were closest by geography to the border with England, but those living in the Scottish lowlands in the 1600's were victimized at regular intervals by raiding highland clans. The soil was thin and rocky, and lacking exposure to the most basic farming techniques, the meager harvests scarcely provided much beyond what was required for next year's planting. Lowland Scots were as poor as the soil was thin. They were often hungry and caught up in regional violence between the many clans, as the settlements of families were called.

Those clans with the largest numbers of young men naturally prevailed as the strongest, and there existed a state of continued infighting among the several ruling clans, which contributed – not only to the general lawlessness – but to an inability to create alliances against common foes, including the English. There were lowland clans, but the majority of the families living in that area south of the Scottish Highlands and the English border; specifically, those residing south of a line from Edinburgh to Glasgow, lived in conditions that could only be termed as squalor.

The terrain was infinitely more accessible than the highlands, but was little improved as to the requirements of agriculture. The best farmland to be found was along the eastern edge of the lowlands, but its proximity and easily-reached landscape made it all the more desirable to raiding parties of both the English and the Highlanders. Elsewhere, land was stony and dotted with marshes and bogs that would have taxed the patience of even the most experienced of the world's farming population.

As a result, Lowlanders planted their gardens on the sloping sides of hills in irregular patches between the rocks and bogs. Their houses were constructed of any material that might be piled up into a wall, mostly blocks of peat and sod that were thatched with grasses. Timber was hard to find, so much so that laws passed in the late 1500's required the replanting of trees, but the laws were not enforced. Visitors to the region penned accounts of the region and the citizenry in terms that might best describe a safari to the remotest regions of the earth.

Towns of the lowlands were little more than collections of families who lived in service to the main landholder of the area, called freeholders or lairds, in an arrangement not far removed from the feudal system of medieval times. Both parties understood the arrangement, and consequently, lowland farmers had scant hopes for prosperity or independence. Tenants used the crudest of instruments to till the rocky earth while acknowledging that Scottish soil was not meant for farming.

They planted seeds to grow a crop known as 'gray oats,' a strain considered unsatisfactory and abandoned by farmers around the world. The oats themselves had little nutritional value, and with the portion paid to the laird and that set back for next season's planting, little remained for consumption.

As an alternative to the tribulations of the farm life, some lowland men left Scotland to join the ranks of soldiers and sailors in the frequent conflicts between European countries. The mercenary Scots served as a thin line of contact between the nascent Scottish civilization and the sophistication of music, art, and progress already in full blossom among the western European countries. For most, the stories were little more than fables and legends, turned into songs to which the villagers might dance during festivals.

The periodic merchant fairs and traveling exhibits offered respite from the commonly held notion that the station of the Scot was predetermined, and that little hope existed for a societal change. It was at the markets that Scots could sample foods that had to have been considered exotic, and view such items as paper and glass.

The home of the Scottish Lowlander was built without such luxuries as glass windows, and the lack of suitable wood prevented the construction of chairs, tables, chests or beds. The irregularly-formed walls, generally only as tall as rocks could be safely stacked without mortar, had gaps filled with mud and straw. The family might sleep on mats of straw and sit on smooth stones that had been brought inside. The cooking fire, which also served to warm the home on cold nights, was built in the center of the structure so the smoke could eventually curl its way through a hole left in the grass thatching of the roof. When the grass and turf of the walls and roof became too dry, the family might simply pull down the stones and rebuild, using the dried materials as fuel for the fire.

Lacking wood for fencing material, a Scottish farmer might build a short stone wall, or – as often as not – simply bring the family cow or pig inside the house at night to keep it from wandering.

It was not only the Scots who lacked the amenities of British civilization; the Irish populace was just as mired in the Middle Ages. With exceptions, both countries were lawless and poverty-stricken hinterlands that appealed only to the hardiest European adventurers, and then only for the short duration of the visit.

In journals that survive those adventurous outings, however, the Scots and the Irish are both portrayed as high-spirited and happy people, who loved music and holidays, dancing and singing. For many Scottish Lowlanders, the great change in their lives came in 1603, with the death of Queen Elizabeth of England, who had campaigned mightily to bring both the Scots and the Irish into the circle of English jurisdiction.

In the years before her death, Queen Elizabeth sent forces to put down a rebellion by two Irish clan leaders, Tyrone and Tyrconnell, who ruled Ulster, the northernmost of the four Irish kingdoms. They were finally subdued and fled Ireland, and the Crown declared their land to be forfeited and ownership given over to the English Crown.

At his ascension to the throne in 1603, King James immediately saw an opportunity to bring about an assimilation of the Irish into the English fold. An edict that declared his "unspeakable love" and affection for his subjects in Scotland opened up land in the Kingdom of Ulster for colonization. Where his predecessor Elizabeth tried to conquer the 'wild Irish,' King James hoped to have them infiltrated by Protestants from Scotland and England. In all, nearly a quarter million acres became eligible for the transplanted Scots, who greatly outnumbered the English subjects taking up the offer starting in 1609.

"The king had a natural love to have Ireland planted with Scots," wrote Stewart of Donaghdee, a Presbyterian minister. "Beside their loyalty, of a middle temper, between the English trader and the Irish rude breeding, [they are] a great deal more like to adventure to plant Ulster than the English."

It was the break the downtrodden Scots needed to overcome the hardships of the Lowlands existence. The "Great Plantation," as it was termed, allowed Scottish families to leave their homeland – many for the first time – for the promised of improved conditions and a better life. Previously, emigration was a huge risk, given that most destinations were greatly removed and would require a substantial financial risk to achieve. Ulster, on the other hand, was practically a stone's throw from their native land, and the risk of failure could be offset by the ease at returning to the former farmstead in Scotland. Added to the lure of improved conditions that prompted moves by the Scots was a new tax implemented by Scottish landowners. The *feu* – as it was called – was a rental fee assessed in addition to a portion of the harvest already being turned over to the lairds. Scots were cash-poor and many were dispossessed of their homes as a result, and the Ulster Plantation represented a lifeline to stability.

Six months after the offer was made, seventy-seven Scottish families applied for grants, but when the tracts were awarded in 1611, the number had been reduced to fifty-nine. Those were accepted as Ulster colonists and were awarded some eighty-thousand acres. Word quickly spread, and the promise of rich soil, bountiful harvests, and flourishing livestock soon began to draw even those Scots who had not been evicted.

Although the English subjects who took up the offer were smaller in number, their presence was significant. From the English, the Scottish colonists were able to learn modern farming practices that had never crossed into the Scottish agricultural practices. Marshy bog lands were drained and opened for cultivation, providing immediate results, and waves of new colonists.

Left behind in the Scottish Lowlands was the woeful grain called gray oats, replaced on the farms of the new colonists by a new crop brought from South America by Sir Walter Raleigh. The resulting harvest was so abundant that the vegetable became known as the "Irish Potato," and became a staple all over Ireland. It was eventually brought to the American colony when Scots-Irish immigrants began arriving there in 1718.

The success of the agricultural efforts in Ulster allowed the new residents to cultivate other causes as well. Presbyterianism – the official religion of Scotland – took on a fervor never before experienced. The religion was a central focus of the community, and the common prosperity allowed for the construction of church buildings at which Sunday services and sometimes day-long meetings were held. Inspired to share the teachings, the transplanted Scots organized public schools, a practice continued in the American colony by the Scots-Irish immigrants in later years.

The Ulster homes were more functional than architectural marvels, with each colonist required to construct a *bawn* – transposed as *barn* – to house the livestock. Homes were largely constructed of rock and featured several rooms as opposed to the single-room sod-walled houses in the lowlands of Scotland. Again, the influence of the British colonists came into play, with many structures featuring elements of English construction.

Few drawbacks existed to the Ulster colonization, and Scottish families continued to make the crossing. Within a decade, Ulster was home to more than fifty-thousand Scots and English colonists, and those who were first to settle later became the first to leave when the 100 year leases came due. [Appendix A]

The families brought enterprise to Ulster in addition to their religion. The region, being suited to grazing of sheep, quickly established itself as a center in cloth making, to the point that the exported product brought world currency to the communities. The new economy allowed for the introduction of trades, and residents were no longer forced to make livings strictly from the land. Shoemakers, millers, carpenters, sheriffs, and tailors could ply their trades on the foundation of the quality wool industry.

That success became part of the demise of the Scottish colonists in Ulster. The Great Plantation, the settling of wild lands of Ireland, underwent a change from its primitive colonial experimental beginnings to a contemporary society that impacted the world trade, all in the course of a single century. By the early 1700's, the English colony in America was well-founded and reports of prosperity were tempting to those in Ulster whose leases were drawing to a close.

In 1717, the "Great Migration" from Ulster to America began, spurred by the English restrictions on the importation of Irish goods, a practice begun in 1671 to overcome the Ulster linen trade competition. It was a series of droughts, however, that diminished the agricultural harvests that felled the growing Ulster economy and forced the beginning of emigration. Beginning in 1714, and for the next six years, insufficient rainfall ruined the Ulster crops and sent the cost of food soaring.

Another ingredient leading to the mass migration was the Test Act of 1703, through which the English attempted to force the Ulster Scots into compliance with the Church of England. That restriction forbade the Scottish Presbyterians and the Irish Roman Catholics from holding civil or military office. Also banned was the practicing of church services, and religious-based teaching – the cornerstone of Ulster public education was outlawed.

The ultimate insult came in the form of lease increases. The initial unimproved land came at a cheap rate on a long-term lease and had been renewed through the 1600's without significant alteration. As thousands of leases came due in the early 1700's, the rental fees were greatly increased on the basis that the now-improved land held a greater value. The Scots, who had created the greater value through their own labors, were reluctant to pay the higher amounts and their leases were turned over to the highest bidders. Often, groups of native Irish banded together to combine resources to cover the lease amounts.

The raised rents were considered price-gouging by the Scottish in Ulster, and American newspapers carried accounts using the term 'rack-renting.' The stories focused on the latest arrival of a ship of immigrating Irish, who began migrating en masse to the English colony in America

CHAPTER TWO

Among the American Colonists

Most of the Scots arriving in the northeastern ports of the American colony were in much better financial shape than their families had been at the initial arrival in Ulster. Descendants of those first Ulster colonists were better off in terms of both finance and education. They might not have all qualified as wealthy, but there were some well-off immigrants among the early arrivals. Newspaper accounts documented entire church congregations departing together for a fresh start across the Atlantic.

For the passage, each passenger could carry a single trunk at no cost with additional baggage requiring payment of a surcharge. Many families sold what they owned in Ulster with the intention of replacing the items once they had settled in the new land. Ship passage could be paid by cash or barter, and some offered themselves in trade in the form of indentured servitude, some choosing the option merely to save the money that would have been spent on the fare for some later use. An indentured servant also was assured of food and shelter by the sponsor, along with a length of time to become acclimated to new customs and surroundings.

For most arrivals, Philadelphia marked the initial port of entry, and colonists there were aware, and somewhat surprised, at the sheer number of immigrants. Robert Gambie of Londonderry wrote a letter that was published in a London newspaper concerning the flight of the Ulster Irish, a piece that was reprinted in the Pennsylvania Gazette.

By 1775, when the Revolution effectively ended the 'Great Migration,' more than a quarter of a million Irish immigrants of Scottish heritage were living on American soil.

The English colony in America had been founded just three years before the Ulster Plantation, and by the time of the migration from Ireland the northeast had firmly established villages and towns. William Penn was among those who had advertised and even journeyed abroad to find suitable residents for the province being settled.

Both the British Crown and colonial land speculators were happy to accommodate those who could help populate the western lands and stem the expansion of the Spanish and French colonies in America. Most Presbyterian Ulstermen hoped to establish farms in the new land and found communities in which to establish their churches. Their options were somewhat limited.

To the south, Virginia and Carolina were already firmly established as Anglican slave-holding plantations, and so the first immigrants from Ulster landed primarily at destinations further north. Maryland and New York were both primarily plantation colonies as well, and not considered suitable destinations. Some early Ulster emigrants wound up in parts of Maryland, but as the tide of arrivals increased in New England, the early welcome they had received was effectively withdrawn. Eventually, ships bound for America from Ireland simply traveled up the Delaware River to Pennsylvania ports. There the immigrants from Ulster found a more sincere welcome.

In his advertisements, William Penn boasted of the wonderful climate of the province, the rich soil, its beneficial geographic location, and a religious tolerance. In 1681, Penn had advised those who were considering his invitation, to consider the expense involved:

> …they must either work themselves, or be able to imploy others. A Winter goes before a Summer, and the first work will be Countrey Labour, to clear Ground, and raise Provision…

There were specific costs listed in his prospectus, *A Brief Account of the Province of Pennsylvania.*

> 1st. The Passage for Men and Women is Five Pounds a head, for Children under Ten Years Fifty Shillings, Sucking Children Nothing. For Freight of Goods Forty Shillings per Tun; but one Chest to every Passenger Free.

William Penn, realizing his recruits would have little knowledge of the basic living essentials that would be required to survive, included in his advertisement a list of suggested items that would make the journey and settlement easier, things such as tools, building supplies, and clothing.

> Lastly. Being by the Mercy of God safely arrived; be it in October, Two Men may clear as much Ground for Corn as usually bring by the following Harvest about Twenty Quarters; In the mean time they must buy Corn, which they may have as aforesaid; and if they buy them two Cows, and two Breeding Sows; with what the Indians for a small matter will bring in, of Fowl,

> Fish, and Venison (which is incredibly Cheap, as a Fat Buck for Two Shillings) that and their industry will supply them. It is apprehended, that Fifteen Pounds stock for each Man (who is first well in Cloaths, and provided with fit working Tools for Himself) will (by the Blessing of God) carry him thither, and keep him, till his own Plantation will Accomodate him. But all are most seriously cautioned, how they proceed in the disposal of themselves.

By the time of the first massive migration of Scots-Irish, the English colonies had a thirty-year history of success. When the Scots-Irish arrived in Philadelphia, they found colonists living in homes of brick and mortar, complete with windows and sashes. Some, like Penn's own home, were comfortably, if not elaborately, furnished. The streets of Philadelphia were well planned, and accommodated sturdy homes, merchant's stores, and office buildings. The areas outside Philadelphia, on the other hand, were much less refined.

Along with his Quaker settlers, Penn had successfully lured impoverished Germans from the Rhinish Palatinate still suffering the effects of the Thirty Year's War. Germantown was founded in 1683 and the German settlements spread westward through what became Chester (later Lancaster) County.

The Scots-Irish would only view the homes in passing as they made their way to the western lands of the province. Indentured servants would remain in the settled areas, but the majority of the incoming Ulster families were seen as an effective buffer between the 'Northward' Native Americans and the settlements of the passive Quakers and the reserved English. Both groups viewed the incoming Scots-Irish as a race of troublemakers better suited to life on the frontier.

The Scots-Irish immigrants had no objections to the idea. Lands along the western frontier constituted everything an Ulsterman could have dreamed, with fertile soil, endless timber for construction, and boundless supplies of wild game.

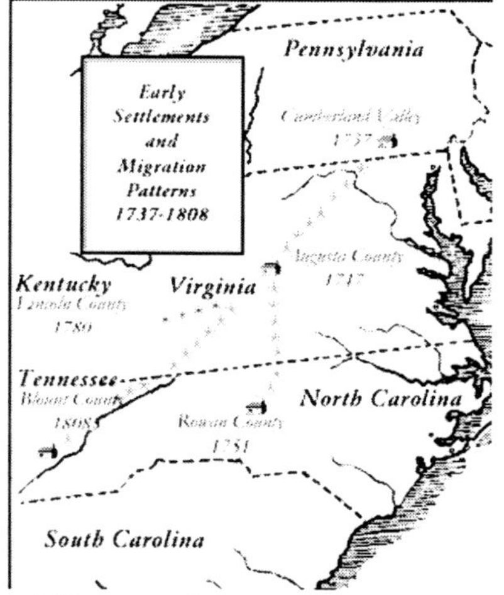

Germans continued to immigrate during the same period as the Scots-Irish flight, and the settlement of the remaining Pennsylvania lands, as well as the rich valleys of western areas of Virginia and the Carolinas, documents the movement of two groups.

As neighbors, the Germans and Scots-Irish could not have been more different. German homes were well-designed and constructed of squared timbers, suiting their desire for permanence. They were industrious, orderly, and dealt well with the native tribes.

Conversely, Scots-Irish builders simply felled trees and notched the ends of the logs before stacking them into walls, filling the resulting gaps with clay or mud. Socially, they were viewed as quick-tempered, given to fancy, and less efficient in their farming habits; some only tilled the sunlit strips between the shades of trees.

The Scots-Irish viewed the various Native American nations as a single group, leading to confrontations with otherwise peaceful tribes. In 1763, during a particularly savage period of hostilities between Indians and colonists, a group of Scots-Irish in Paxtang Township in Dauphin County raided a Conestoga settlement and murdered twenty members of the tribe in the surprise attack.

There were occasional feuds between the Scots-Irish and the Germans as well, but generally, they cohabitated on the colonial frontier with a tolerance for the other's presence.

The first significant Scots-Irish settlement was on the eastern shore of Maryland, beginning in 1649. By 1682, Somerset and Calvert counties featured five Presbyterian meetinghouses. The accounts of those earliest immigrants from Ulster encouraged many others to emigrate.

It has been estimated that between 1717 and 1718 more than five thousand Scots-Irish made the move to America. There were four subsequent waves of migration: 1725-29, 1740-41, 1754-55, and 1771-75. The numbers are not exact, but as many as fifteen thousand may have immigrated between 1725 and 1729, and by 1790, an estimated 454,000 Americans were immigrants from Northern Ireland, comprising over 14 percent of the total population.

An Ulsterman himself, James Logan was Secretary of the Pennsylvania Province, and was among the first to extend an invitation to his Scots-Irish countrymen. After a time, he became disenchanted with the idea.

Logan's perception of his Scots-Irish countrymen as men who had "bravely defended Londonderry," led him to offer lands nearest the "Northern Indians." Ten years after the first settlements in Chester County, Logan wrote that five Scots-Irish could cause him more trouble than fifty other men. He eventually denied grants, but it only caused other troubles.

The Scots-Irish saw land as free to claim, and some former indentured servants established "squatter's rights" as a means of saving money. Logan estimated in 1726 that those with no rightful claim had settled over one hundred thousand acres of the frontier.

Some attempts were made to enforce legal settlements and measures were sometimes extreme. Frontier cabins were burned as a show of force, with little practical effect.

The Scots-Irish simply rebuilt as their ancestors had done. British subjects preferred the Scots-Irish illegally on the frontier, as opposed to living among them as less than desirable neighbors.

Illegal squatters constituted only a portion of the Scots-Irish colonists. Donegal was filled with deeded Scots-Irish landowners, living to the south of the deeded Germans. Provincial papers from Chester County list the sale of 200 acres of land to William Stephenson in 1734. Others in the Donegal region of present-day Lancaster County included a great many Scots-Irish who settled the area in the early part of the eighteenth century. [Appendix B]

On the east side of the Elk River, in Cecil County, Maryland, there were four deeded Alexander families. By 1740, Cecil County Alexander families included those of James, William, Moses, Nathaniel, John, Joseph, David, and Theophilus. William Stephenson, arriving in 1672, was also among those preceding the first 'wave' from Ulster.

Most of the Scots-Irish in Pennsylvania had been farmers in Ulster, and on arrival, sought farmland. Penn's advertisements offered five thousand acres for one hundred pounds. Renters paid a penny an acre for fifty acre tracts. Prices escalated as the desirable lands became scarce. The Cumberland Valley was filled with Scots-Irish settlers by 1734, when Samuel Blunston of Wright's Ferry was given permission to sell land licenses. David Houston, applied and received a land grant for 320 acres in 1737, and settled on Conococheague Creek along with a great many other Ulster families. [Appendix C]

The Scottish faith also found an early foundation, with the establishment of the Rocky Spring Church and five others in the Cumberland Valley between 1734 and 1740.

Before the end of the decade, the Scots-Irish farms were well established in the Cumberland Valley. Rough farmhouses would acquire amenities and comforts over time. News of any sort could only be had from travelers along what was called the Philadelphia Wagon Road or the Great Wagon Road.

In 1749, the French began posting signs through the Ohio Valley, some near Pennsylvania, in attempt to establish rights of ownership. By 1753, the French were using alliances with Native American nations to provoke attacks on English settlements beyond the Alleghenies. The conflict eventually extended into the valleys of Virginia and the backcountry of North Carolina inhabited by Scots-Irish in Rowan County. [Appendix D]

CHAPTER THREE

The Shenandoah Valley

Just beyond Swift Run Gap in the Blue Ridge Mountains is a magnificent and fertile valley, nestled in between the Appalachians and the Blue Ridge. An explorer trekking through the backcountries was overwhelmed by the beauty of the valley beyond, and called the region the Euphrates. His label became forgotten in favor of a Native American term meaning "Daughter of the Stars." Shenandoah Valley's rich soil, grassy plains, and forested hills, became an important destination for a great number of Scots-Irish immigrants.

When the rich lands became available beginning in the first half of the 1700's, many Scots-Irish were quick to undertake the journey, and the majority of those comprised a third wave of Ulster emigrants to America. They barely hesitated in Pennsylvania before heading for the lands of "Shenando." Others who headed for the Virginia frontier were established Scots-Irish families with younger members who were ready to start their own households and found land prices had become too expensive in Pennsylvania.

Governor William Gooch, in 1730, granted forty thousand acres of choice Virginia land to John and Isaac Van Meter of Pennsylvania. The Van Meters almost immediately sold the extensive tract to Joist Hite, who built an estate and brought in a number of families to join him. The first settlers made homesteads two miles south of present-day Staunton in Augusta County, Virginia, in 1732.

Two later grants added additional lands for settlement, attracting a large number of primarily Scots-Irish families to the province. William Beverley was given 118,491 acres in Orange County for the "Manor of Beverley," a tract that extended into what is now Augusta County, Virginia, which developed into one of the most predominately Scots-Irish settlements in America. Benjamin Borden of New Jersey was given a land patent in 1739 for 92,100 acres that included the southern part of present Augusta County and nearly all the present Rockbridge County lands. Borden was required to have one hundred settlers on his tract before he could receive title, a feat he accomplished within two years. He attracted so many Scots-Irish settlers in the process that the land grant came to be called the "Irish Tract."

Borden was able to quickly settle the area, in part, due to his friendly dealings with squatters who had already established themselves in the new territory. Since authorities over the region were nearly two hundred miles away, men on the frontier had to apply their own brand of legal practice; a "corn right" entitled a man to a hundred acres for each acre he planted, a "tomahawk right" declared that trees felled and marked with indicated property lines, and a "cabin right" was understood to declare ownership of surrounding land for the builder of a cabin. Until the administrators of the land grants arrived to oversee the allotment of farms, the frontier "rights" provided for a way to settle disputes among the earliest settlers in the Shenandoah Valley of Virginia.

Augusta County was formed in 1738, but it wasn't until 1745 when the organization meant anything, since previous to that there was no courthouse, no records, no sheriff, and no justices of the peace.

John Stephenson, along with brothers Thomas, David, and William Stephenson, were among the early settlers of the Shenandoah, arriving in the northern area in 1740. They along with others who were looking for an area that would better accommodate their Presbyterian faith, found rich farmland in the Shenandoah Valley.

In the 1720's, the Great Wagon Road originally reached only from Philadelphia to the settlements in Lancaster County, and at its frontier end, where the trees and undergrowth were thickest, it would hardly accommodate a wagon. As the frontier extended, the Pennsylvania end of the trail was beaten down into a colonial highway of sorts. As the country's primary road heading south, the Wagon Road crossed through York and Gettysburg and by 1760 extended all the way to Salisbury, North Carolina – a distance of more than four hundred miles. Lancaster, PA became the starting point for many colonists, and eventually, traffic was so great that the settlement became an important trade center and one of the last stops before the long haul toward Virginia.

The lands along the Wagon Road were as beautiful as they were rugged. Travel for the Scots-Irish heading for the frontier was usually in groups consisting of several families, since safety was better insured in larger numbers. Attacks from Native Nations were still a genuine threat; it wasn't until 1744 that a temporary peace was achieved through the signing of the Treaty of Lancaster.

The Shenandoah Valley had long been considered tribal hunting ground and consisted primarily of lush prairie, due to the planned burning of grasslands at the end of the hunting season. The annual prairie fires promoted the heavy growth of new grass the following season, and the resulting stands attracted large herds of buffalo.

The forest at the edge of the valley was thick with brush and grasses and wildlife was not confined to the squirrels and birds. It was the heavy hooves of buffalo that stamped out the first traces and deer were plentiful. Panthers still roamed the southeastern forests and could pose a threat to frontier families, along with bears, bobcats, and poisonous snakes. The wolves, most of which had never encountered a man, had not yet learned a need for fear, and were so brazen that they were initially undeterred by the sound of a gunshot.

A gun was required for travel. The Scots-Irish called the tool a rifle-gun, and most preferred the long-barreled weapon called the Pennsylvania Rifle. It was just one of the many items each traveling party could find at the village of Lancaster before taking up the Wagon Road. The flintlock was a modified European gun with a barrel over forty inches long, and was treasured as one of the primary tools of the colonists on the frontier. Even with its primitive firing mechanism, it served both as a source of protection and a provider of food and clothing. Equipped with the long rifle, an ax, salt, seed, and sewing items, a family could draw from the land all the things needed to make a home. It was not uncommon to have a colonist's "rifle-gun" mentioned in a prominent fashion in his last will and testament.

The early settlement of the Shenandoah Valley occurred at a time when quick thinking, horse sense and a little ingenuity were not only admirable, but also required, for survival. Anything that needed to be done had to be done by the family. When the Scots-Irish settlers reached the Virginia valley, there was no hotel to accommodate them while their homes were built, no warm bath in which to soak after the long trip. There were no workmen waiting to take up the hammer. It would take days, cutting the trees, notching their ends and stacking them, to achieve the barest of shelters. Those arriving later might be afforded some shelter by neighbors with completed houses; lacking neighbors, the family would have to sleep under the stars, if at all. A number of the early settlers complained that the howling of the wolves was so distracting they were unable to sleep.

John Stephenson was the earliest settler in the Mill Creek Valley of the Shenandoah, receiving a patent in 1741 for 760 acres of land located just south of present-day Harrisonburg in Rockingham County. His arrival is among the many recorded in surviving court documents.

> 22nd. May, 1740: John Stephenson came into court and made oath that he imported himself, Sarah and Mary Stephenson from Ireland to Philadelphia, and thence to this colony.

His brother Thomas declared importation the same day, also naming his wife Rachel. The Mill Valley they chose for their settlement was a fertile creek bottom with a breathtaking view; at the base of the Peaked Mountain in the Massanutten Range, three creeks wound their way toward the Shenandoah River. Cub Run, Mill Creek, and Stony Lick Branch (later called William's Run) all provided impressive settings for the valley pioneers, most of whom desired that the neighbors be friendly – but located a fair distance down the road.

The western slope of the Massanutten is drained by the North Fork of the Shenandoah, with the mountain rising between the north and south forks. The settlement chosen by the John Stephenson was about midway between the lands of William Beverly and Jost Hite, to the south and north, respectively. John and his wife Sarah lived about fifteen miles east of the land homesteaded by John's brothers. Thomas, David, and William patented land in the Mossy Creek-Mount Solon area of Augusta County, some fifteen miles southwest of present-day Harrisonburg.

Five brothers moved from Delaware to settle the region around present day Harrisonburg – John, Daniel,

Thomas, Jeremiah, and Samuel Harrison. Daniel Harrison received a patent August 20, 1741 for a tract of 400 acres on Dry Fork of Smiths Creek (about two miles north of present-day Harrisonburg). The holdings of the Harrison brothers constituted a huge percentage of the land in what later became Rockingham County. Although the land patents issued to both Daniel Harrison and John Stephenson were dated 1741, both men were in the Shenandoah Valley along with several others, several years previous to the official deeding of the land.

Germans emigrating from the economically depressed Rhinish Palatinate in Europe made up a sizable percentage of the settlers in the northern region of the Shenandoah, but the Cross Keys area (south of present-day Harrisonburg, and the site of a Civil War battle) was a settlement primarily populated by the Scots-Irish. John Craig and his wife Sarah took up land on lower Cub Run. William and Janet Craig, and their son John, homesteaded some two miles south of Cross Keys near Robert and Jean Hook. Near Good's Mill on the same creek was William Williams. Robert Scott built on the North River near present-day Port Republic. Patrick Frazier bought land on Stony Lick Branch, as did Robert Shanklin. The Mathew Thompson Senior and his son Mathew Junior made homes on Stony Lick Branch near the North River. James Laird, who later led a militia company from the area, built a home for his wife and three children at the headwaters of Cub Run, near the base of Peaked Mountain. Nearby were William and Mary Beard, and the home of Samuel Scott.

There were three families with homes on the headwaters of Mill Creek, those of John Stephenson, Archibald Huston, and James and Catherine Waite. The families eventually comprised two sets of "in-laws" who located in close proximity near Cross Keys, and exemplify the frontier patterns regarding marriages based on need and proximity. Archibald Huston wed Stephenson's daughter Mary, and John Stephenson was married to Sarah Waite, the daughter of James and Catherine. After the death of Sarah, John Stevenson married her sister Esther, who was the widow of John Taylor. Times required that a woman have a husband, and it was nearly equally necessary for a man, particularly with children, to have a wife. Marriages between widows and widowers were fairly common.

When John Stephenson completed construction of his plantation house on Mill Creek, he called it "Meadow View" – a name that would endure for more than 250 years. As more travelers passed Meadow View, the trace became a road – first called the Indian Road, for the nearly constant moving of native tribes along the path during the signing of the Treaty of Albany in 1740. It was later called the Courthouse Road, and finally named the Keezletown Road. Shortly after the Revolution, a Scotsman named John Loudon McAdam invented a process using tar and asphalt to bind small stones together for the surfacing of roads. The Keezletown Road was the first in Rockingham County to be given a macadam surface, and in the early years of western Virginia settlement, the road served as the main route of north-south travel through the valley.

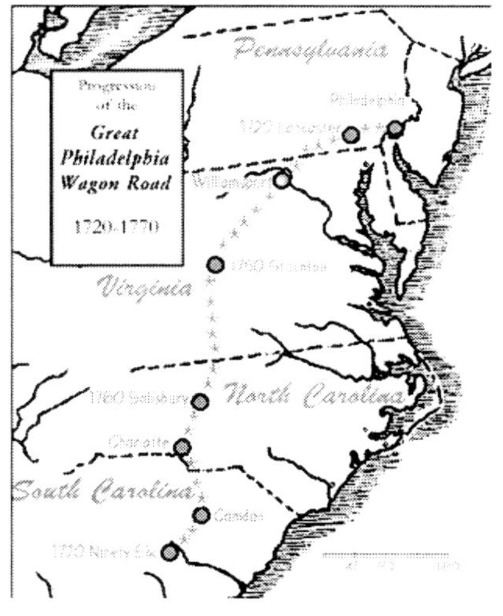

The first homes, particularly those far from the towns and stores, were simple structures intended as immediate shelter. Tables and three-legged stools were pieced together from branches and pieces of wood; pegs were driven into the interior walls to hang the few articles of clothing and the flintlock. Spoons for cooking and eating had to be carved, as did the serving bowls and ladles, unless a gourd or hard squash was to be found. It was only much later that dishes and drinking mugs began to appear, bartered for from wandering merchants; any guest served a meal on pewter or china would leave for home much impressed at the affluence of his host and hostess.

The majority of those moving into the Virginia valley had just crossed the Atlantic, leaving most of their possessions behind in Ulster, but as removed as the Scot-Irish were, simple pleasures could be maintained. A horse racing track was established across the road from the Meadow View plantation house in 1746, and is believed to be the first track to be built in America west of the Blue Ridge Mountains. While many of the early settlers enjoyed their horses, it was a sticking point among the hard-liners of the Presbyterian Church.

Augusta Church, founded in 1740, was the first Presbyterian Church in the valley. The church house served as headquarters for the community of people, a gathering place for social and spiritual events. New Providence Church was another early congregation, and a church building was constructed at Cross Keys, an area seven miles south of present-day Harrisonburg. Massanutten Cross Keys is located on the old Keezletown Road just south of the old Port Republic Road. At the time the meeting house was constructed, Henry Downs Junior lived at the location of present-day Port Republic, and on May 29, 1751, Henry was appointed Surveyor of the Highway from his house to the "Stone Meeting House." When the old Port Republic Road was established from "Henry Downs' Mill to ye Meeting House," Thomas Stephenson was appointed as overseer for its upkeep.

Later, many of the members of the Peaked Mountain congregation petitioned the court for a new road running from just west of Swift Run Gap (near present-day Elkton, Virginia) "in a westerly direction joining the court house road at the New Stone Meeting House." [Appendix E]

One of the earliest preachers in the Valley became fast friends with the settlers, literally as well as figuratively. John Hindman emigrated from County Londonderry in Ulster to serve as a missionary among the newly planted Scots-Irish. He was preaching in the Shenandoah Valley as early as 1742, and records of the Donegal Presbytery indicate Hindman was preaching "at the head of the Shenandoah" (near present-day Port Republic) in 1745. The Presbyterians had no church in the area other than the Peaked Mountain Church at Cross Keys (later called the Massanutten Church), and Hindman is believed to have been its first preacher.

The Reverend Hindman was comfortable not only in the pulpit, but in the saddle as well. An avid horse racing fan, he owned a large stable of his own horses and jockeyed the mounts at Stephenson's track. When the Presbytery objected to Hindman's participation and he declined to give up the sport, the church excommunicated him in 1747. Hindman opted to be ordained as an Episcopalian minister, and at his return, he was elected the first rector of the Augusta Parish, giving some of the more moderate Presbyterians in the valley an option in their church affiliation. He was taken gravely ill less than a year after his return from England, and died at John Stephenson's Meadow View.

The Reverend Hindman's will included a collection of wigs and gowns, divinity books, twenty-three horses and a "jockey coat and cap." His was one of the early graves at the Cross Keys cemetery, the burying ground for the Scots-Irish congregation of the Massanutten Church. Records survive of that early congregation. [Appendix F]

Frontier life presented a common need for defense, and communities met the need by forming militia companies that drilled semi-regularly. In truth, they were simply farmers with rifles under the command of one of their peers, elected as the captain out of respect or experience. Among the Scots-Irish in Virginia, militia captains in Augusta County included James Cathey, John Christian, Peter Scholl, John Smith, Charles Campbell, John McDowell, Andrew Lewis, John Willson, and John Buchanan. The presence of Peter Scholl as a militia leader is evidence of the German population in the county.

The men of the time were expected to provide food and shelter for the family, keeping the house in good repair and tending to the farm, as required. To acquire those things that could not be grown or made, the men would have to barter or sell something to raise the money. The women of the time had little legal standing. Those who found themselves widowed on the frontier or those not adequately provided for, were completely dependent on relatives. Few widows managed farms on their own, although there are accounts of frontier women who proved to be shrewd businesswomen following the deaths of their husbands. More often than not, widowed women hoped to remarry before their inheritance was expended, which assumed that provisions were made in that regard.

Many frontiersmen died without making a will, although the early legal books are filled with the last intentions of the more conscientious. Most were respectful and caring, and many were quite meticulous in providing for their widows and "orphans" as the children were termed – regardless of whether the mother was still living.

Others were not as kind. John Hood Sr. willed that his several thousand dollar estate be generously divided among his children. His spelling was lacking, but his intentions were clearly spelled out. His daughter "Sophiah" received $153 dollars worth of property in addition to "a negro girl Dabney valued at $700," but the said "property" was to be "in nowise the property of Moses Moore her husband." To his widow Mary, John

Hood left "one silver dollar as she as Bin so stubron with Me so carless of Me & so neglet full of mine."

The women were expected to raise the children, make the clothing, and prepare the meals. Naturally, cooking was done over the fire, but the type of cooking depended on the utensils available to the family. An iron spit was used to roast meat over the flames, and since the side of the cut nearest the flame tended to overheat, a member of the family – usually one of the younger children – was required to sit at the fire and turn the spit. The resulting meal, not unlike modern cookouts, might have equaled modern efforts, recalling that there was no understanding of sanitation or correct methods of food-handling at the time.

Not surprisingly, there were settlers who lacked even the most basic of cooking utensils. There were others who had the basics, but not much else. John McClure worked as a tailor, but the income was limited and his life's accumulation resulted in a rather thrifty inheritance for the family. To his son James, he left "the Bible and the big pot." Son Samuel McClure received "the next biggest pot." John realized his family had to eat, and not wanting to overlook his widow, declared "wife Agness to have use of both pots." Sons John and Andrew, along with daughters Eleanor, Jean and Esther were left – without a pot, or the use of one.

Those who were fortunate enough to own an iron pot or two could boil meat and vegetables to provide a variety of meals for the family. The practice of baking was limited to those who could improvise or those who owned a bake kettle. The heavy covered pans came in a variety of sizes and shapes, but were usually equipped with legs to allow the pan to be placed directly among the embers. Red-hot coals were piled on top of the kettle, which allowed food inside to be baked.

The wife and daughters were expected to serve the men their meals, and many preferred to eat alone afterward, rather than trying to serve and eat at the same time.

Beyond the church and the family, social activities were fairly limited for the Scots-Irish in Virginia. Part of the reason was the strict Presbyterian discipline, in which dancing and other frivolities were strictly forbidden. Even the serving of hot coffee on Sunday was frowned upon by the strictest Presbyterians. There was much to keep the colonists occupied without a busy social calendar, but like any other community, there were those who weren't as skilled at putting time to good use. James Houston found himself in a scrape, along with his friends David Bryans, Israel Robinson, and James Bullock, when their hunting trip ended with a woodland blaze. Although the hunt was successful, the outcome was less than desirable; Houston was charged with killing a deer, setting the woods on fire, and swearing in public.

There was little tolerance among the Presbyterians of Augusta County for rough language. Swearing in public was an offense punishable by fine – the amount dependent on the severity of the curse. Fines and fees declared by the county were used to subsidize the cost of county salaries and supplies.

Since the Scots-Irish preferred the civilized social amenities of church and community, there were positions such as Constable and jailer to be filled. As residents of a new county, Augusta citizens found themselves with a list of tasks required for the good of the community, many of which required funding. The colonists appear to have shouldered their financial obligations with an understanding as to the need. The court appointed overseers and those "tithables" within their districts were required to perform civic work, or pay an equivalent amount of "Current Money." The designation of currency was due to the variety of payment methods available; most of the provinces issued their own currency, and even those were subject to change.

When Staunton became the county seat, the courthouse became a center of activity during the monthly sessions. Construction began on a jail in late 1746, and a guard was hired to secure the "prison" until it was finished. Robert McClenahan was obliged to find candles and small beer (a beverage low in alcoholic content), and to keep the court house in order, besides finding stables for the horses of the Justices, attorneys, and the Officers.

Colonial times were not without scandal. Sometime in 1746, Humberston Lyon and Susan Mires, the wife of William Mires, were suspected of conducting an illicit love affair, and both faced adultery charges in court.

That trial paled in comparison to the Buchanan scandal, beginning in the early part of the following year. Much of the county was swept up in a murder trial beginning in April and those who were not called to take the stand filled the courthouse to watch as Rebecca Buchanan faced murder charges. Her mother Rebecca (referred to as Rebecca Senior), along with Ruth Buchanan Carmichael, and Mary Ann Campbell were charged on "suspicion of being accessories," and many of the county wives apparently knew something about the death and the purported conspiracy. More than a dozen persons took the stand to testify against the four, referenced in court documents as "criminals." The younger Rebecca was bound over for trial at Williamsburg, while the three accused accessories were all acquitted on May 20.

A good amount of the county activity was the direct result of the monthly court sessions, and landowners were required to petition for the establishment of new roads and improvements. If the court agreed to the need, men would then be obliged to assist in the clearing and maintenance. Residents petitioned for a road from Caleb Jones' mill to the County line, and more than two dozen Scots-Irish settlers were ordered to maintain it. The court even made decisions on such things as road direction signs that were set up along the county roads.

In the early years of Augusta County, the focus of activity was on farming the land and furnishing the needs of the colonists, although farming was not the only livelihood in August County. Entrepreneurs were quick to spot the need for enterprises such as grain mills. If the gristmill was to be run by water, and the miller had none on his property, he could petition the court to condemn a suitable piece of land. The court appointed a jury of men to survey the value of the land and return with an appropriate amount of compensation for the landowner.

The court appointed men to serve as appraisers, as estate sales were a common practice following a death. Neighbors were asked to witness the sale of land and the filing of wills at the courthouse. During monthly sessions, men were called to serve on juries, although serious offenses were sent for trial at Williamsburg. Not all the jurymen were practiced in the art. Walter Davis and Malcolm Campbell had their fill of the trial in which they had been assigned a seat on the jury. Suddenly, Walter bolted out the door and Malcolm leaped out the courthouse window. The court noted it was forced to stay a verdict, since the two "separated themselves from their fellows and talked with other persons."

Marriages on the frontier were occasions for great celebrations, and lacking other amenities, generous gifts of land were often given to the newlyweds. Among the Scots-Irish in Augusta County, much of the land would later be sold as families followed the frontier into Kentucky.

CHAPTER FOUR

Western Carolina Country

Whatever arguments settlers might have had among themselves, they were in agreement about the beauty of the frontier's rugged geography. Beyond the Shenandoah Valley, heading southward along the Blue Ridge Mountains and crossing at the Manassas Gap, travelers on horseback saw wide valleys that were thickly carpeted with grasslands and colorful flowers. Where the Yadkin River and the Catawba River basins coursed through the western part of North Carolina, herds of deer roamed through grasses that grew so tall that a rider on horseback could tie handfuls of it together across the top of his saddle. Originally, they were Granville's lands.

Of the eight Lords Proprietor of Carolina, all but one sold their holdings to the crown in 1728. John Carteret, Earl of Granville, retained his share, stretching from the Virginia border to fourteen miles southwest of present-day Salisbury, North Carolina. John Lawson, an early day trader who traveled extensively through the Granville district, reflected on the beauty of the Carolinas that would serve to draw settlers to its fertile meadows.

> A man...may more easily clear ten acres of ground than in some places he can one; there being much loose stone upon the land, being very convenient for making of dry walls or other sort of durable fence...we passed through a delicious county – none that I ever saw exceeds it. We saw fine bladed grass six feet high along the banks of these pleasant rivulets...This most pleasant river is beautified with a numerous train of swans and other sorts of river fowl, not common though extraordinary to the eye.

Between 1732 and 1737, many of the colonists living along the boundary between Maryland and Pennsylvania had grown so weary of the provincial border disputes they began to move away. Many sought lands in the Shenandoah Valley, others settled in the Cumberland, and still others pressed onward, eventually reaching the Carolina frontier. Recent immigrants and those unable to afford the farms in Pennsylvania joined them on the journey along the Great Wagon Road. A fifty-acre farm in Lancaster County of present-day Pennsylvania sold for an average of seven pounds ten shillings, while one hundred acres in the Granville district could be had for a mere five shillings. The North Carolina frontier also had an appeal to colonists from New Jersey and Pennsylvania in 1744, areas under threat of attack from the Indians allied with the French during King George's War.

By 1749, much of the choice land in the Shenandoah Valley had already been claimed as well, and the frontier was pushed into the Yadkin River Valley of North Carolina. That same year, Anson County was formed in western North Carolina, and the provincial council considered eighty petitions from settlers seeking land in the new county. Most of the earliest settlers headed large Scots-Irish families. They joined – however tenuously – the established inhabitants of the region; the Keyauwee, Saponi, and Tutelo Indians lived in the valley between the Yadkin and Catawba Rivers, and the Catawba and Waxhaw Tribes lived west of the Catawba, to the south of the other tribes.

Grants for land parcels to the Scots-Irish and other settlers within Granville's tract used geographic features to mark boundaries, and surveys included such references as "on the N side of McColloh's Line on both sides of Bufflow Creek beginning at Hickory runs E 220 poles to a white oak."

The initial use of a simple rope or cloth for taking measurements gave varying results, since the length of the rope was dependent on its age and condition. An old wet rope might give a settler a significantly larger piece of land, once stretched. To offset that possibility, surveyors carried metal poles, sometimes called chains, of a determined length, that fastened together at the ends similar to the links of a chain. The poles could be neatly folded at their links, stashed in a long pouch or saddlebag, and easily carried through the wilderness.

The Catawba River is in the western part of the state, running east from present day Pisgah National Forest near the Tennessee line to a point just northwest of present day Charlotte, where it turns south. The county situated in that basin was called Anson, with a presumed western boundary at the Mississippi River, or beyond. Later, a more reasonable western line was set, and over the years, Anson County was eventually carved into 26 smaller counties. Changes in county lines were often the result of petitions by colonists, who were forced to travel great distances to conduct business.

The Yadkin-Catawba River valley constituted one of the largest primarily Scots-Irish settlements in America.

There were several major areas of settlement when the first wave of Scots-Irish moved onto lands originally claimed by Sapona and Catawba tribes. The Fourth Creek Settlement comprised fertile lands east of the Catawba River, on the upper reaches of Third Creek and Fourth Creek. The Davidson's Creek Settlement was established as colonists made homes along the branches of Davidson's Creek, east to Coddle Creek. The Irish Settlement and the Trading Camp Settlement were found between the Yadkin River and Lord Granville's Line. By 1753, there were just over three-dozen landowners in the Yadkin River area. [Appendix H]

William Morrison called himself the "first Inhabiter of the country," although there were others who might take issue with his claim. The Morrisons were certainly among the early residents of the Carolina backcountry, and settled near John McConnell in the Davidson Creek settlement. William Morrison had a mill in operation by 1752 and built a house on Third Creek, on land he bought in November of 1753 in present-day Iredell County.

As had been the case in Pennsylvania, not all of the settlers taking up land on the frontier of North Carolina had established a valid title to the land.

On the first day of April, a meeting of the Governor's Council was held, and it was pointed out that a number of those who had petitioned for land had never taken out a warrant to have it surveyed, and others who had completed a survey, had never returned with the information to complete the land patent. Whether it was a matter of purposely avoiding the payment of fees, or simply an oversight on the part of colonists, they found their names listed at the Council Chamber, along with a notice requiring that the patent application be completed within eight months time, or rights to the land would be forfeited. In light of the fact that people were pouring into the area, legal rights to property were becoming increasingly important. Many of the settlers had been living for up to four years on the Granville tract without legal claim, and the Council notice set in motion a rush to establish rights.

48 individual grants for land in North Carolina were made on a single day – March 25, 1752. It may have been because it was New Year's Day, the last time it would be celebrated in March. Unlike the Roman Catholic countries, England and its colonies kept the Julian calendar, in which the New Year was marked on March 25th. On September 2, 1752, the colonists lost nearly two weeks – on the calendar, at least – when the Gregorian calendar was adopted. September 14 was the day that followed September 2. [Appendix I]

Third Creek Church - Rowan Co. NC

While most who applied for land were seeking a place to settle, there were a number of known land speculators, some of whom grew prosperous dealing in the sale of land. Not all the deals were honest. There are accounts of lands being sold more than once, and of failures to properly record deeds on behalf of new owners. Either way, land went quickly in Rowan County, and mostly went to "transfers" – colonists who had established a previous home in Pennsylvania or Virginia, and were removing to the Carolinas.

The rich bottomland of the Yadkin and Catawba Rivers was advertised to the Scots-Irish, much in the way the Virginia valley was marketed years earlier. North Carolina Governor Gabriel Johnston had come from Dumfrieshire,

Scotland, and the man who took the seat in 1754, Arthur Dobbs, originated in Ulster.

Between the years of 1752 and 1755, the Centre Presbyterian Congregation was established in the Davidson's Creek settlement area, placing the Scots-Irish at the edge of the Carolina frontier, and establishing the earliest organized settlement to be found as far west as the Catawba River.

By the time Dobbs visited the area in 1755, seventy-five families had already settled. Dobbs owned several large tracts of land nearby, and was pleased at the progress made by the frontier families. He reported that most contained eight or ten children each, and that some "Scotch-Irish Presbyterians" had banded together to have a preacher and a schoolteacher of their own.

Acting Governor Mathew Rowan wrote in 1753 that, only seven years earlier, there were not more than "one hundred fighting men," a number "now at least three thousand." The number of fighting men was a general concern, since colonists were still under the threat of attack. The so-called French and Indian War had several phases, and there were almost constant reports of incidents in North Carolina from 1753 to 1760. During that period, skirmishes were often close to home for the Scots-Irish; a raiding party of French and "Northward" Indians was met by a contingent of Catawbas less than two miles from the Rowan Courthouse, resulting in a battle in which more than half of the French and Indian group was killed.

The Catawba Tribe had been on good terms with colonists until the middle part of the 1700's. Perhaps frustrated by the influx of white settlers into their traditional territories, they began to take up the ways of the more hostile Nations and staged raids on colonists.

Governor Dobbs decided the threat to settlers was real enough to require protection, and ordered the construction of a fort, to be located west of Salisbury. By

January of 1757, the three-story fort was under the command of Captain Hugh Waddell, whose company of forty-six soldiers was enough to convince the Cherokees to end their hostilities – at least temporarily.

Casualties were not as severe for North Carolina colonists as they were during the same period in Virginia's Shenandoah Valley, where some 68 persons died during attacks over the course of two years. In those early years, before officials addressed the safety of the colonists, the Scot-Irish had to depend on their own wits and the aid of their neighbors, just to stay alive. Many others determined it wasn't worth the risk, and moved to lands east of the Yadkin River. The population of Rowan County dropped nearly half between 1756 and 1759, when only 800 taxable persons were counted.

Two major roads eventually passed near Salisbury, which began as a tiny settlement and after a short time became a major trading center for colonists in the backcountry of North Carolina. From the eastern parts of the province, travelers could take the Trading Path west to Salisbury, or if heading southward from Pennsylvania and Virginia, the Great Pennsylvania Wagon Road, which extended through Salisbury, and eventually south to Charlotte and beyond. The earliest residents of Anson County had to create their own roads.

Many of the Scots-Irish farmers preferred living at the frontier, where a good days hunting could provide much more for the family than tending a garden. Many persisted in the belief that areas of land on which no trees grew represented barren soil, and as a result, declined to plant in the meadows. Planting among the trees forced the clearing of land to allow sunlight to penetrate. The Scots-Irish farmers were often content to chop down as few trees as possible and then girdle the rest at the trunk. When the trees eventually died, the trunks were hauled away, but the rows of corn were forced to detour around the numerous tree stumps dotting the gardens. A tree stump near enough to the house could serve a practical purpose. The center was hollowed out until a hard depression was formed in the trunk. In the bowl of the trunk, corn could be pounded into meal.

Although there were others, corn, tobacco, and flax were among the primary crops grown by the Scots-Irish. When flax was grown, it could be made into coarse linen that was tailored by the women into clothing.

Even during the summer months, it was a common sight to see long trails of smoke rising from the rock chimneys of the homes throughout the country. The fireplace on the frontier burned constantly, for cooking and for the warmth it provided. There were no panes in most of the settler's windows, which were covered with cloth or hides. As a result, to allow sunlight into the cabin in winter also brought in gusts of cold air.

Isolated as they were, the Scots-Irish quickly discovered that when the corn crop was brought in, haste was essential in preserving the harvest. Corn was used in the feeding of livestock; it was ground into meal, and was served at the table – but what was not immediately used quickly rotted where it was stacked. Markets were too distant to allow the practical hauling of produce, and as perishables, the crop was of limited value in bartering with others.

Rather than let the corn go to waste, most farmers found that a simple process would preserve the harvest through an entire winter. In addition, processing the corn insured a constant value and allowed the harvest to be easily transported. That process was distillation, and in the days before temperance became a social agenda, whiskey from the "still" was considered "God's Gift." Not only was it viewed as a remedy for aches and pains and an aid to good health, distilling the corn mash purified it of the bacteria that perpetrated the "summer discomfort" brought on by spoiled milk and the water of many wells and streams.

There was drinking to excess among some, but most residents of the colonies simply took a quick nip or two at various times throughout the day. Even the strict Presbyterians had little problem with the practical use of whiskey.

For a wedding, the bride's father was expected to provide gallons for the ceremony, which usually lasted throughout the day. Before the dancing and merry-making got into full swing, two of the younger men would race to the bride's cabin to fetch the jug of "Black Betty." The winner of the foot race got to carry back the prize, and he, along with his defeated opponent, would run – leaping and yelling like madmen – back to the ceremony. Once returned, the winner was allowed the first kiss of the new bride, and – with great ritual – the groom was handed the jug of whiskey. After his quick swig, the container would then be passed around the room. It was a semi-formal ceremony of calling the toast, and as each was handed the jug he called to the crowd, "Health to the groom! ...not forgetting myself!"

In the community of Carolina plantations, weddings were among the few diversions. The shivaree, as it was called, was the wedding party that extended well into the evening, and included escorting the bride and groom to their bed, with much joking and laughing. Once the newlyweds were sufficiently attended, the crowd returned outside and began a tremendous ruckus, beating together anything that made a decent noise, and calling out taunts to the newlyweds. Often, the bride could end the celebration by promising a meal or party the next day. It was the unfortunate bride who attempted to silence the crowd, which would only clamor all the longer and all the louder at her pleadings.

Horseracing was another popular diversion, and many times betting occurred, even among the Scots-Irish Presbyterians, although swearing at the losing horse was strictly forbidden. Another popular pastime was a game called "long bullets," in which a large iron ball was moved by one team toward a goal, defended by the other team, a sort of cannonball soccer. Later, many communities outlawed the game, citing its disruptive nature along the streets and roads.

Among the frontiersmen in western North Carolina life gradually became less about solitary struggles in the wilderness, and more about co-existing with the ever more numerous residents, in addition to the rigors of life on a farm. Crops had to be planted and harvested. Livestock required tending. Meat had to be cured for storage. Cloth was woven, shoes were made and tools repaired. When families began moving into areas that became Charleston and Salisbury, cattle and other livestock were sold or bartered with merchants who had opened shops. Bounties for wolves were paid at Salisbury, and it was there colonists who preferred the hunt could find a ready market for deerskins.

Hugh Parks and James Huggen bought property on the Catawba River, and near the forks of Dutchman, Cedar, and Cubb Creeks, while Squire Boone sold his Buck's County land to Edward Milnor in 1730, and moved his family to Philadelphia County. In 1750, after a brief time in the Shenandoah Valley, the Boones settled in the Yadkin river area of western North Carolina, establishing a home on Bear Creek.

Descendants of the Boones and other Yadkin Valley Scots-Irish would meet again in the wilds of Kentucky, chasing the frontier beyond the Cumberland Gap.

CHAPTER FIVE

Frontier Conflicts

Scots-Irish settlement was well underway in the Shenandoah Valley and in the backcountry of the Carolinas when the Ohio River Valley became the center of attention on two continents. At the time, that region was considered by colonists to be part of the Province of Virginia, although the area nearest the headwaters of the Ohio is that lying in present-day western Pennsylvania.

Virginia land speculators, already successful in luring settlers to the South, began eyeing the American interior, lands which were claimed by the French, the English, the Iroquois, and the Province of Virginia.

The Ohio Land Company of Virginia was formed in 1749 and obtained two hundred thousand acres south of the Ohio River, with the promise of additional land as soon as one hundred families moved into the area. Eight hundred thousand acres were allotted to the Loyal Land Company to the west, in the area historically recognized as Indian lands.

With strong settlements in Canada and Louisiana, the French intended to span the distance in between with forts and missions along the Mississippi River and through the Ohio Valley. Lacking the colonists to establish settlements, the French governor of Canada dispatched Captain Pierre Joseph Céleron de Blainville in 1749 to stake claims of ownership through the area.

Word of the French expedition quickly traveled through the frontier and Scots-Irish landowners in the Cumberland Valley at the time were relieved when news arrived that the French traveling party turned to the west. They anticipated trouble and families were forced to consider relocating.

Robert McKitrick lived at Jenning's Gap in Virginia. His daughter Isabella was standing in the front yard when a group of young men approached along the road. She recognized Andrew Fowler, and called to him as he neared. Andrew spoke as he walked, and told Isabella that they intended to join the army to fight the French at Fort Duquesne.

A land bounty would await each volunteer who served in the effort. Years later, after Isabella was married and went by the name Isabella McGlamery, she spoke of their encounter that day, before a court hearing intended to sort out the various land bounty claims. An Augusta County contingent that was comprised mainly of Scots-Irish joined the expedition along with Andrew Fowler and his companions in the excursion that became known as Braddock's War. [Appendix J]

The British had every intention retaking the Ohio Valley, and determined two regiments of British regulars could easily accomplish what a militia force led by George Washington had failed to do. General Edward Braddock, a sixty-year-old career soldier, was sent to conduct the campaign.

Along with the British 44th and 48th Regiments, members of the colonial militia from Virginia and North Carolina began gathering for the impending battle. George

Washington had resigned his command, but offered to serve without pay as an advisor to Braddock.

There were twenty-five hundred men behind Braddock when he left Fort Cumberland, Maryland in June. Travel through the dense forest took so long, that he opted to detach fewer than fifteen hundred of his best men to advance more quickly on Fort Duquesne, while the remainder continued the march as reinforcements. In leading the column, Braddock envisioned a quick victory over the 800 French at the fort. His failure to account for the Native American style of combat led to his defeat.

The French suffered less than sixty casualties. For the British, the losses were massive. Only 459 of the 1,373 privates escaped uninjured, and over 60 of the 86 officers were killed or wounded.

General Edward Braddock died two days later, and Washington ordered his burial in an unmarked grave in the middle of the trail, to disguise its location.

England was shocked at the fall of Braddock to what was considered a lesser force, and Virginia fell into a panic. The frontiers of Virginia and the Carolinas, primarily settled by the Scots-Irish and the Germans, were under the immediate threat of attack.

Many in the Shenandoah Valley chose to abandon their homes rather than face the continuing threat of Indian attack, and others were simply driven from their land. Governor Morris of Pennsylvania wrote in November of 1755, "What a vast tract of country has been depopulated by these merciless savages."

In western Pennsylvania, some estimates had reduced the number of fighting men in the area from 3000 to a mere 100. Many more opted to remain, facing those who would drive them from their lands with a characteristic determination.

Descriptions of the Scots-Irish tenacity contain common threads in regard to their apparent fearlessness. They were called "fighters – wherever courage, activity, and force were wanted – they had no equals." Many of the traits later used to describe Americans in general are the same as those used in describing the colonial era Scots-Irish frontiersman. The bold fighter, quick-tempered, God-fearing, righteous, defender of the faith, was the Scots-Irish frontiersman.

It was their ferocity as fighters during the times of continual raids that established them a place when they were newcomers in the colony, and the more pacifistic of their neighbors viewed them as a positive line of defense against attack. The Scots-Irish demeanor – although liable at times to provoke confrontations – was respected when the protection of the settlements was concerned, and it served to lessen the time the Scots-Irish were cast as interlopers in the British colony.

It is an unfortunate aspect of human conflict that compassion and decency as regards the other side are quickly lost. The tribal members who battled to preserve their ancestral lands and the Scots-Irish, who fought to protect the homes they had built in the wilderness, were both guilty of the most vicious types of warfare.

Winthrop Sargent, a historian who wrote of Braddock's expedition, described the Scots-Irish: "Impatient of restraint, rebellious against anything that in their eyes resembled injustice, we find these men readiest among the ready on the battlefields of the Revolution. If they had their faults, a lack of patriotism or of courage was not among the number. Amongst them were found to be men of education, intelligence, and virtue."

There are accounts of ministers preaching sermons with a gun next to the Presbyterian prayer book in the pulpit, mindful of the possibility of attack even as services continued. It was largely the contributions of the Scots-Irish on the colonial frontier that brought about the eventual ending of the French holdings in the Ohio Valley.

Augusta County militia members serving in the French and Indian Wars were among those who later took land bounties in Kentucky. William Dangerfield was allotted 2000 acres in Jefferson County, and other grants went to William Bronaugh, Mordecai Buckner, Thomas Buford, Timothy Conway, William Fleming, John Fox, Nathaniel Gist, Peter Hogg, William Hughes, Stephenson Huston, Charles Lewis, George Mercer, George Muse, James Samuel, John Savage, Charles Scott, Robert Scott, John Smith, and John Thompson, all of whom served from Augusta County, Virginia.

—

While Braddock was making his ill-fated march to Fort Duquesne, Governor Dobbs of North Carolina was making an expedition of his own. In written remarks to the Board of Trade, Dobbs described his trip to the western edge of the province, and mentioned the Yadkin river as "a large, beautiful river where is a ferry. It is near 300 yards over, it as at this time fordable scarce coming to the horse's bellies. At six miles distance I arrived at Salisbury, the county town of Rowan. The town is but just laid out, the courthouse built and seven or eight log houses erected."

Among those seven or eight houses were four that served as public inns. Even as the guns were firing on Braddock at Fort Duquesne, settlement of the Carolina backcountry was in high gear. Those who came to settle in what was now Rowan County, having been divided from Anson County in 1753, could find food and lodging while they constructed homes on their land. Public inns were busy places and already the proprietors faced some stiff regulation by county officials. "Spiritous Liquors" were to be sold at the rate of six shillings per gallon, and small beer for a penny per quart. Even the fare at the inn came under the scrutiny of the county court.

> Each Dinner of Roast Boiled flesh 8 pence Brakefast and Supper four Pence each Pasturing for Each for the first 24 hours 14 pence and for Each 24 hours afterwards 2 pence, Stableage each 24 hours with good hay or fodder 6 pence.

The bed, which may have been enjoyed by the weary traveler regardless of condition, was "a good Bed and Clean Sheets Two Pence."

Colonists in North Carolina were also facing somewhat frequent attacks by tribes, included the Catawbas, a Nation previously on good terms with the settlers. William Morrison advised the county that several had come to his mill and tried to throw a pail of water into his meal trough. He reported that when he tried to stop them "they made many attempts to strike him with their guns over his head."

Rowan County settlers gave 500 Pounds in "proclamation money" to buy guns and ammunition. James Carter and John Brandon were entrusted with the money, but the cash proved too great a temptation for Carter. He was accused in 1757 of misappropriation and was fired as Justice of the Peace. He was expelled from his Assembly seat and resigned his commission as Major in the militia. Brandon might have faced sanctions as well, but died in the interim period between the raising of the money and the discovery of its misuse.

Diplomatic efforts brought a temporary peace with the Cherokee Nation, and as a result, many of the settlers serving at Fort Dobbs began returning to their homes.

By November of 1758, only Jacob Frank and one assistant remained at the fort. Frank was a German settler who owned one of the early inns at Salisbury. The fort was no sooner abandoned than attacks on settlements resumed by the Cherokees in North Carolina.

In 1758, British fortunes on the frontier began to change. British General John Forbes was sent to take Fort Duquesne. He left the site of present-day Bedford, Pennsylvania with five thousand provincial troops and fourteen hundred Scottish Highlanders. In September, eight hundred of the Highlanders were sent ahead to scout the fort and wound up in a fierce battle with tribal warriors. Both sides lost nearly a third of their parties.

Hugh Waddell, an Ulster émigré, left his command at Fort Dobbs to join in the Ohio Valley fighting against the French and Indians. He returned in early 1759 to head a small contingent of Scots-Irish militiamen. Before attacking Fort Dobbs, tribal warriors killed Robert Gillespie of Rowan County, and the fourteen-year-old son of Richard Lewis. A short time later, Waddell, back at Fort Dobbs, noticed activity around the fort, and headed a party of ten men to investigate the matter. In a letter to Governor Dobbs, Waddell indicated his force was greatly outnumbered.

> We had not marched 300 yards from the fort when we were attacked by at least 60 or 70 Indians. I had given my party orders not to fire until I gave the word, which they punctually observed: we received the Indians fire: when I perceived they had almost all fired, I ordered my party to fire which we did not further than 12 steps each loaded with a bullet and seven buck shot, they had nothing to cover them as they were advancing either to tomahawk or make us prisoners:

The remainder of the tribe attacked the fort and met with similar fire. Waddell reported 10 or 12 of his enemy killed or wounded, and "on my side I had 2 men wounded one of whom I am afraid will die as he is scalped, the other is in a way of recovery and one boy killed near the fort whom they durst not advance to scalp."

Colonial militias retaliated for the attack on the fort, and Colonel Alexander Osborne, Captain Martin Pfeiffer, Captain John Kerr, and Captain Conrad Michael were among those leading men against the warring Nation. David Houston served in Osborne's primarily Scots-Irish company, with Lieutenant John McWhorter and Ensign Zebulon Brevard.

Fifteen Native American villages were destroyed during a two-year campaign that pushed the tribes westward to the foothills of the Appalachian Mountains. Terms of a treaty reached between the colonists and the Cherokees intended to establish a boundary line between the two groups, but it was a treaty forced upon the Cherokees, who had few other choices. With the French vanished from the Ohio Valley, the English and their colonists had no further use for the tribes earlier courted as allies.

CHAPTER SIX

Insecurities of the Frontier

To call it a peaceful life would have been extravagantly optimistic and a good deal misleading regarding the frontier settlements and plantations of the Scots-Irish. The fanfare and ceremony that marked the acquisition of French holdings by the British may have been too far removed from the colonists in Virginia and the Carolinas to make any impression.

After abandoning Fort Duquesne, the French fled their western forts as well. For the most part, by 1760, the British were in possession of virtually all of Canada. On the frontiers of Pennsylvania and Virginia, the signing of the Treaty of Paris in 1763 may have raised hopes that the violence of the previous decade had ended. In the agreement, France ceded all of its holdings east of the Mississippi, including Canada, to Britain.

It may have been the original religious tenets of the Presbyterian Scots-Irish and an adherence to the practices that brought them from ignorance and poverty in Scotland to having attained some degree of respectability in the American colonies – over the short term of two or three generations. Whatever the reasons, the Scots-Irish settlers were ready users of the colonial courthouse, and their lives are amply documented in the archived papers of the time. Even those men who had little to declare set aside the time to put on paper a last will and testament, and the religious foundation of the Scots-Irish was almost always noted in their final depositions. Typical wills began with such affirmations as "I give my soul into the Hands of God, who gave it, and for my body I recommend it to the Earth to be buried in a Christian manner...nothing doubting but at the time of the Resurrection I shall receive it."

It was also customary to disperse through an itemized list such items as dishes and plates, pots and pans. Generally, land went to the eldest son, but those with ample holdings could disperse lands in tracts.

Wills of the period, particularly those involving men of some means, generally mentioned the disposition of slaves. Some, but not all, Scots-Irish held slaves during the period. It was also a common practice that furniture and like items, generally termed the "movables," that were not specifically mentioned in the will, were sold at a public vendue, or sale.

Often, the widow was placed in the position of having to buy back from the estate any items she wished to keep that were not specifically mentioned in the will. Bequeathing items to the widow that presumably were her own, such as kitchen utensils or clothing was also a common practice. It is a rare will of the period that acknowledges possession of articles by the wife, especially items owned before the marriage.

When the estate of William Adair was listed, one of the larger private libraries of the county was made available, and its titles give an indication of the reading material of the time: Watt's *Philosophical Essays*, a medical dictionary, *Bailey's Dictionary*, *The Art of Surgery*, *Confession of Faith*, *Death and Heaven*, *The Interest of England*, *Psalm Book*, *Durban on*

Death, The Wars of England, The Free Nonconformist, and an arithmetic book.

In the matter of the estate of Alexander Anderson, the legal activities included the authorizing of payment for six gallons of peach brandy consumed during his illness and at his funeral.

As early as 1762, there were at least 62 families living south of the Yadkin River along the outreaches of Third and Fourth Creek in western North Carolina's back country. Most were Scots-Irish, and many had been in the colonies for a number of years before relocating to the Carolinas.

Thyatira Church - Rowan Co. NC

Andrew Morrison was an early settler, dating to 1762, and his property was located in the west part of present-day Rowan County. Nearby property owners were John Kerr, Benjamin Wiley, Robert Morrison, Michael Bird, James Knox, John McElwaith, and David Morrison. Hugh Waddell bought land just north of the Fourth Creek Meetinghouse in 1756 from John McCulloch, who owned, but never lived on the land.

John Jack moved from Chester County, Pennsylvania to settle as one of the pioneers in the fertile savannah between the Yadkin and the Catawba rivers. John Potts and James Potts moved into the area from Maryland at about the same time. Between the forks of the Yadkin and South Yadkin rivers and Lord Granville's Line to the south was one of the larger settlements in western North Carolina. It was so populated with Scots-Irish that it became known as the Irish Settlement. They were primarily farm families and were largely content in bypassing elected or appointed public office. The town of Salisbury was laid out just north of the center of the Irish Settlement.

It was in Salisbury in 1763 that a change was in store for Elizabeth Gillespie. Her husband Robert had been involved in a business venture with Thomas Bashford, and their enterprise had become quite successful. Robert Gillespie was scalped and killed during a Cherokee attack in 1759, and the following year, his widow bought a lot in Salisbury from William Williams to operate a public inn.

She apparently possessed a business savvy that equaled that of her late husband, and over the next two years, Elizabeth became one of the continent's early female business success stories. She later bought a second lot in Salisbury, and a 275 acre tract of land adjacent to the town proper. She ran the public house and managed the land purchases alone for three years, until she married William Steele, a recent emigrant from Pennsylvania who bought sixteen lots that adjoined Elizabeth Gillespie's property at the north edge of Salisbury.

Together the couple prospered, and raised a son – John Steele – who became a public figure in his own right, then serving the young state of North Carolina in the legislature and as a member of the first Congress of the United States. President George Washington appointed Steele as the first Comptroller of the Treasury, and he served in that capacity until 1802. The same year Elizabeth Gillespie remarried, more than 150 people were living in Salisbury and more than 74 of the original 256 lots laid out had already been sold. There were houses, shops, inns, a doctor, lawyers, a candle maker, three hatters, a butcher, a tailor, a wagon maker, and two general stores.

The Presbyterian congregations of the Scots-Irish met at Thyatira Church, which was one of the focal points on the western fringe of the Irish Settlement. John Thomson was a Presbyterian preacher, and among the first to minister in the northwest part of the province. Before the meetinghouse at Thyatira was constructed, he conducted frontier services at the homes of William Morrison, Osborne's meetinghouse, Cathey's place, and Samuel Young's settlement – later, the site of the Fourth Creek Church.

Changes in the frontier community were also reflected in the variety of community offerings among the Scots-Irish. A small library was kept at Thyatira Church, where volumes such as Butler's *Analogy of Natural and Revealed Religion*, and Mosheim's *Ecclesiastical History* could be referenced. A classical school called Crowfield Academy was established near the home of Alexander Osborne. Pupils at that school included Adlai Osborne, Aaron Houston, Samuel Eusebius McCorkle, and Ephraim Brevard, the son of John Brevard. Ephraim Brevard became involved politically and served as secretary in a group that composed a treatise that for years was called the "Mecklenburg Declaration of Independence."

While residents of tidewater Virginia continued to view those in the west as backward farmers, life in the Shenandoah had advanced significantly from its crude beginnings. Unlike the "Irish Settlement" in North Carolina, where many of the Scotch-Irish had just arrived and had small farms and little money, many in the Virginia valley managed much larger farms.

While the term plantation used interchangeably with the word farm, some of the Shenandoah properties were large enough to justify the term. The Harrison brothers managed huge operations in Rockingham County, and opted to use slaves to assist in the field work. John Stephenson, without the typical large Scots-Irish family, took on both slaves and indentured servants to assist in the operations.

CHAPTER SEVEN

The Scots-Irish Militia

When John Murray, the fourth Earl of Dunmore, became Governor of Virginia in 1772, one of his first official travels took him along Braddock's Road to Fort Pitt on the western frontier. Dunmore was a brash, outspoken man and had bold designs for the Province of Virginia. At Fort Pitt, Dunmore persuaded Dr. John Connally to act as his agent in a scheme to establish a more northern boundary for the Virginia colony. The Governor had already made an impact on the area, by issuing land grants in the Ohio Valley to veterans of the French and Indian campaigns, although the grants were in violation of treaties negotiated with the Shawnees and other tribes.

Connally posted an announcement at Pittsburgh in January of 1774, informing of his appointment to the position of "Captain, Commandant of the Militia of Pittsburgh and its Dependencies," although shortly after the posting, Connally was arrested by Pennsylvania justices and was held at Hanna's Town, near present-day Greensburg. Connally persuaded the justices to release him, on a promise that he would return in April, when the next court would be convened.

In early spring, the Shawnees, who were most affected by the encroachment of Dunmore's veterans, began attacking the settlements. Volunteers were sent by Dunmore to reinforce those living in the troubled area. Meanwhile, another group of militia was sent with Connally in April when he returned to Fort Pitt, and the 175 militiamen arrived "with their colors flying," and the captains with "their swords drawn." He took possession of the fort and renamed the outpost Fort Dunmore. The following day, April 8, three Pennsylvania justices who lived near Fort Pitt, but were in session at Hanna's Town, returned home, where Connally had them arrested.

The border dispute was only part of the conflict; Dunmore called on the Scots-Irish militiamen to counter the Shawnees who were raiding colonial settlements, and authorized the movement of several companies under the command of General Andrew Lewis. It became known as Dunmore's War – a brief but vicious campaign that involved some fifteen hundred militiamen against the Shawnees. That Nation was alone in facing the colonial militia, after unsuccessfully attempting to bring in the Iroquois as allies.

The Scots-Irish had pushed the frontier well into Shawnee territory in present-day Virginia and Tennessee's Holston River valley. As early as 1772, the Scots-Irish crossed the New River west of the Iron Mountains in southwest Virginia, and cleared land at Wolf Hills for a settlement. Another twelve miles to the west, Captain Evan Shelby staked a site, and to the south, in what is now Tennessee, other Scots-Irish banded together for the purpose of self-defense and self-government, naming the collective the Watauga Association. It was at the onset of Dunmore's War that the Pennsylvania rifles and their owners were forced to defend themselves against the Shawnee's retaliation for the loss of their ancestral lands.

Daniel Boone and Michael Stoner were sent by Virginia authorities in 1774 to warn settlers in the Watauga and surrounding regions that Dunmore intended to attack the Shawnees. On September 24, 1774, the Shawnees attacked the cabin of John Roberts on Reedy Creek. Roberts, his wife, and three of their four children were killed. Their son, the lone survivor of the attack, was taken prisoner. The raid occurred in the jurisdiction of the redheaded Scots-Irishman, Arthur Campbell, a major in the Augusta militia.

When the boy was found scalped – but alive – the troops carried the lad to Campbell's home at Royal Oak, just east of the Scots-Irish settlement, where he was able to describe the massacre, but died of his injuries shortly afterward. The southern raids were originally attributed to the Shawnee, but Campbell soon learned otherwise. He struggled to protect settlers along the Tennessee–Virginia line while Dunmore ordered other Virginia companies to a point some eighty miles to the north.

Dunmore made his way through the wilderness into present-day West Virginia and made camp on the south banks at the juncture of the Ohio and the Kanawha Rivers on October 5, 1774. John Stephenson led a company of militiamen from Augusta County, Virginia. [Appendix L] Officers serving under him included Robert Bell, Benjamin Harrison, George Shilling, John Morgan, Robert Vance, and Jesse Wheeler.

The place where the men made camp came to be called Point Pleasant, a dramatically ironic name, given the wild emotions of the following morning. The Shawnee warriors were led by their chief, Cornstalk, and silently crossed the Ohio at daybreak, catching the militiamen by surprise. The men sprang to arms and flew into a lengthy battle in which both colonists and Shawnees fell at an alarming rate. The skirmish lasted throughout the day, and by late afternoon the colonists held an advantage. When the sun finally set at Point Pleasant, the Shawnees were defeated, at a cost of some fifty men among the militia and a similar number among the Shawnees. Records indicate another 150 colonists were wounded.

Dunmore arranged terms with the Shawnees that allied them with the British and Dunmore himself remained loyal to the crown. Ironically, the militiamen who had served under him against the Shawnees would – almost to a man – fight against the British as colonial militiamen.

The attacks on the southern Scots-Irish settlements were the result of a vengeance-minded Mingo chief called Logan, who turned south instead of joining with Chief Cornstalk in the finale of Dunmore's War. The Mingos believed militia Captain Michael Cresap was behind a murderous attack and when the Shawnees were defeated, the Mingos refused to sign the treaty. Their chief sent a message through Dunmore's emissary:

> I appeal to any white man to say if ever he entered Logan's cabin hungry and he gave him not meat; if ever he came cold and naked and he clothed him not? During the course of the last long and bloody war, Logan remained idle in his camp, an advocate for peace. Such was my love for the whites that my countrymen pointed as I passed and said: "Logan is the friend of the white man!"...Colonel Cresap, the last spring, in cold blood and unprovoked, murdered all the relations of Logan, not even sparing my women and children. There runs not a drop of my blood in the veins of any living creature. This called on me for revenge. I have sought it. I have killed many. I have fully glutted my vengeance.
>
> For my country, I rejoice at the beams of peace; but do not harbor a thought that mine is the joy of fear. Logan never felt fear. He will not turn on his heel to save a live. Who is there to mourn for Logan? Not one!

His defiance of Dunmore is often quoted as one of the finest examples of Native American oratory of the time. The revenge he achieved gave a brief respite for those Scots-Irish in the Holston Valley, including Arthur Campbell, who remained in the area and watched as a steady stream of new frontiersmen passed before his door on the trail to Kentucky.

The Cumberland Gap as Depicted in *Harper's Weekly* 1863

In the final month of 1774, Dunmore ordered county records at Staunton, in Augusta County, be removed to Fort Dunmore. The new jurisdiction was called the District of West Augusta and encompassed much of present-day western Pennsylvania. A new commission of the peace was formed and its first court term was held February 21, 1775.

Daniel Boone always seemed to be on the move, and in March had taken on the task of cutting a path through the Cumberland Gap into Kentucky. He was to soon discover that Dunmore's treaty was no guarantee of peace.

Southwest of the Scots-Irish settlement, Boone and his brother Squire, along with thirty recruits, hacked through the mountainous forests for nearly two weeks. Several acquaintances from the Yadkin River area of North Carolina joined Boone's party, including Colonel Richard Callaway, and Captain William Twetty's Rutherford County militia company: Samuel Coburn, James Bridges, Thomas Johnson, John Hart, William Hicks, James Peeke, and Felix Walker.

After fourteen days of chopping underbrush, trees, and cane, the party emerged from the mountains and camped among the trees south of present-day Richmond, Kentucky – just fifteen miles from their intended destination. Exhausted and relieved, the men slept through the night, without sentry, only to be surprised before daybreak by a band of Shawnees. Boone and his men were surrounded and gunshots rang out in the pre-dawn darkness as the Shawnee warriors fell on the campsite. Twetty was hit in both knees and could not run with the others, who scattered wildly into the woods. Squire Boone grabbed his rifle, but missed his powder horn, and could only drag the useless gun at his side as he crawled through the underbrush.

After several wild minutes, Daniel Boone rallied the men out of hiding and managed to drive off the Shawnees. Unable to continue with two wounded men – Felix Walker was shot in the hip, in addition to the injury to Twetty – Boone had the men hastily build a small enclosure of stacked logs. Twetty died several days after the raid, and was buried at the site. Walker survived, and was carried for twelve days to a place that was later called the "Colony of Transylvania."

It was weeks later that the frontier skirmishes took on a different light, with news of the British attacks on April 19, 1775, at Lexington and Concord. Shortly thereafter, Dunmore, ever the Loyalist and therefore concerned for his safety, retreated with his family to a British man-of-war on the Chesapeake.

Four days before the attacks on Lexington and Concord, Benjamin Logan was striking out on a thin trail leading away from Daniel Boone's crude road. Logan was the son of David Logan, another Augusta County Scots-Irishman, and he was searching for a suitable location to build a "plantation house" for Anne Montgomery, his wife. The two were among the Scots-Irish settlers at Wolf Hills in the Holston Valley.

The point where he left the path is near present-day London, Kentucky, and the trail Logan followed from there to the Falls of the Ohio made up the final leg of what was called the Wilderness Road. Logan was joined by William Gillespie, and the two were following as carefully as possible a nearly hidden trail – or *trace,* as they were called – that had been made by three Scots-Irishmen who had already spent a good amount of time in Kentucky. The trail was Skaggs' Trace, named for Charles, Henry, and Richard Skaggs. It was the aim of Logan and Gillespie to follow the path of the three brothers as long as they could before eventually branching off to explore the Dick's River area. After working their way through hilly forests, the pair finally emerged to find a rolling valley filled with wild crab apple trees. It was a spot that had been used by hunters, and when settlers later followed Logan's path and began settling throughout the grove, it was called Crab Orchard.

After a restful stay of several days, Logan and Gillespie again pushed on, moving through the grassy valleys bounded on one side by rugged hills. The ground was fertile and suitable for planting, and a stream wound its way through the valley, providing needed water. It was the spot Logan intended to build his plantation; the settlement came to be known as Stanford, the seat of present-day Lincoln County, Kentucky, although it wasn't the first name for the community. A Welshman, who was one of

Logan's first visitors, mentioned that May first was the day a Welsh monk was canonized as a saint, and since Logan founded his settlement on that day, the settlement should be called St. Asaphs. Logan is said to have agreed with the idea, but the name did not stick, and the settlement was commonly referred to as Logan's Station.

Frontiersmen sent word for a meeting among the various settlements, and Alexander Spotswood Dandridge, John Floyd, John Todd, and Samuel Wood represented Logan's Station as delegates to what was called the Transylvania convention.

Logan brought his family out the following spring, and by that time there was already a community of Scots-Irish settlers.

CHAPTER EIGHT

Scots-Irish Revolution

Charlotte had been founded as a town in 1767, located in North Carolina's newly-formed Mecklenburg County. It had become a major traffic area for travel south of Salisbury to South Carolina and also had become a center of population and commerce. As the county seat, Charlotte became a natural gathering point for settlers in the area, and when the news of the day was to be heard, someone standing on the courthouse steps called out the latest in a loud voice.

Mecklenburg County residents were holding a meeting in mid-May, when a rider burst in among them carrying news of the attacks by the British at Lexington and Concord. The excited crowd settled at last, and in discussions among the convention principals, including Thomas Polk, Abraham Alexander, Hezekiah Alexander, John McKnitt Alexander, Dr. Ephraim Brevard, John Phifer, Waightstill Avery, and Rev. Hezekiah James Balch, a decision was reached to form a committee to write a response.

The outcome of the efforts of that committee – the so-called Mecklenburg Resolves – is a document that has been debated since that day – with such illustrious citizens as John Adams and Thomas Jefferson weighing in on the discussion. The debate centered on the purported existence of a paper called the Mecklenburg "Declaration of Independence," said to have been written more than a year before the official American document of 1776, and to contain similarly worded phrases throughout.

There is an acceptance of the idea that a convention met at the courthouse in Charlotte and named Ephraim Brevard as head of a sub-committee along with Colonel William Kennon, an attorney from Salisbury, and Reverend Hezekiah Balch. The three were to compose a response reflecting the attitude of the citizenry.

According to tradition, the group labored long in preparing a set of resolves, finally returning to the convention with the document. The crowd at the courthouse had steadily increased, and the group buzzed in anticipation, until at last, Ephraim Brevard began speaking. At once, the room fell silent, as the resolutions were read aloud by Brevard. When he finished the oration and looked up, the room erupted in cheers and applause, and the measures were unanimously adopted. The following day at noon, Colonel Polk read the Resolves from the steps of the courthouse before a gathering of the county residents, and his delivery again met with cheers from the colonists.

Tradition holds that the group voted to have the Resolves carried by messenger to the Continental Congress. Captain James Jack, of Charlotte, was prevailed upon to ride to Philadelphia with a copy of the document, to be presented to the Carolina delegation.

When he arrived at Salisbury a short time later, court was in session there and those assembled compelled Jack to read the document, which he did to a supportive response. Two attorneys, however – John Dunn and a Mr.

Booth – claimed the Resolves amounted to treason and moved to have Captain Jack detained. Tradition holds that Jack drew his pistols and threatened to kill anyone who tried to keep him from his duty, then raced from the courthouse to his horse and spurred his way onward to Philadelphia.

It is said that, upon word that men had attempted to stop Jack, a party of armed men rode to Salisbury for retribution. Dunn and Booth were brought before the Mecklenburg committee; Dunn convinced the group to let him return to Salisbury, and George Graham and Col. John Carruth escorted Booth to Camden, South Carolina. That action has been described by some county patriots with a degree of seriousness as the first military expedition from Mecklenburg County in the Revolutionary War.

The *South Carolina Gazette and Country Journal* is said to have printed the following resolutions:

Charlotte-town, Mecklenburg County, May 31, 1775

This day the Committee of this county met, and passed the following Resolves:

WHEREAS, By an Address presented to His Majesty by both Houses of Parliament, in February last, the American colonies are declared to be in a state of actual rebellion, we conceive; that all laws and commissions confirmed by, or derived from the authority of the King or Parliament, are annulled and vacated, and the former civil constitution of these colonies, for the present, wholly suspended. To provide, in some degree, for the exigencies of this county, in the present alarming period, we deem it proper and necessary to pass the following Resolves, viz.:

I. That all commissions, civil and military, heretofore granted by the Crown, to be exercised in these colonies, are null and void, and the constitution of each particular colony wholly suspended.

II. That the Provincial Congress of each province, under the direction of the great Continental Congress, is invested with all legislative and executive powers within their respective provinces, and that no other legislative or executive power, does, or can exist, at this time, in any of these colonies.

III. As all former laws are now suspended in this province, and the Congress have not yet provided others, we judge it necessary, for the better preservation of good order, to form certain rules and regulations for the internal government of this county, until laws shall be provided for us by the Congress.

IV. That the inhabitants of this county do meet on a certain day appointed by this committee, and having formed themselves into nine companies (to-wit), eight in the county, and one in the town of Charlotte, do chuse a Colonel and other military officers, who shall hold and exercise their powers by virtue of this choice, and independent of the Crown of Great Britain, and former constitution of this province.

V. That for the better preservation of the peace and administration of justice, each of those companies do chuse from their own body, two discreet freeholders, who shall be empowered, each by himself and singly, to decide and determine all matters of controversy, arising within said company, under the sum of twenty shillings; and jointly and together, all controversies under the sum of forty shillings; yet so as that their decisions may admit of appeal to the Convention of the Select-Men of the county; and also that any one of these men shall have the power to examine and commit to confinement persons accused of petit larceny.

VI. That those two Select-Men, thus chosen, do jointly and together chuse from the body of their particular company, two persons property qualified to act as Constables, who may assist them in the execution of their office.

VII. That upon the complaint of any persons to either of these Select-Men, he do issue his warrant, directed to the Constable, commanding him to bring the aggressor before him or them, to answer said complaint.

VIII. That these eighteen Select-Men, thus appointed, do meet every third Thursday in January, April, July, and October, at the Court-House, in Charlotte, to hear and determine all matters of controversy, for sums exceeding forty shillings, also appeals; and in cases of felony, to commit the person or persons convicted thereof to close confinement, until the Provincial Congress shall provide and establish laws and modes of proceedings in all such cases.

IX. That these eighteen Select-Men, thus convened, do chuse a Clerk to record the transactions of said Convention, and that said Clerk, upon the application of any person or persons aggrieved, do issue his warrant to one of the Constables of the company to which the offender belongs, directing said Constable to summons and warn said offender to appear before the

Convention, at their next meeting, to answer the aforesaid complaint.

X. That any person making complaint upon oath, to the Clerk, or any member of the Convention, that he has reason to suspect, that any person or persons indebted to him, in a sum above forty shillings, intend clandestinely to withdraw from the county, without paying such debt, the Clerk or such member shall issue his warrant to the Constable, commanding him to take said person or persons into safe custody, until the next sitting of the Convention.

XI. That when a debtor for a sum below forty shillings shall abscond and leave the county, the warrant granted as aforesaid, shall extend to any goods or chattels of said debtor, as may be found, and such goods or chattels be seized and held in custody by the Constable, for the space of thirty days; in which time, if the debtor fail to return and discharge the debt, the Constable shall return the warrant to one of the Select-Men of the company, where the goods are found, who shall issue orders to the Constable to sell such a part of said goods as shall amount to the sum due; That when the debt exceeds forty shillings, the return shall be made to the Convention, who shall issue orders for sale.

XII. That all receivers and collectors of quit-rents, public and county taxes, do pay the same into the hands of the chairman of this Committee, to be by them disbursed as the public exigencies may require; and that such receivers and collectors proceed no further in their office, until they be approved of by, and have given to, this Committee, good and sufficient security, for a faithful return of such monies when collected.

XIII. That the Committee be accountable to the county for the application of all monies received from such public officers.

XIV. That all these officers hold their commissions during the pleasure of their several constituents.

XV. That this committee will sustain all damages that ever hereafter may accrue to all or any of these officers thus appointed, and thus acting, on account of their obedience and conformity to these Resolves.

XVI. That whatever person shall hereafter receive a commission from the Crown, or attempt to exercise any such commission heretofore received, shall be deemed an enemy to his country, and upon information being made to the Captain of the company in which he resides, the said company shall cause him to be apprehended, and conveyed before the two Select-Men of the said company, who, upon proof of the fact, shall commit him, the said offender, to safe custody, until the next sitting of the Committee, who shall deal with him as prudence may direct.

XVII. That any person refusing to yield obedience to the above Resolves, shall be considered equally criminal, and liable to the same punishment, as the offenders above last mentioned.

XVIII. That these Resolves be in full force and virtue, until instructions from the Provincial Congress, regulating the jurisprudence of the province, shall provide otherwise, or the legislative body of Great Britain, resigns its unjust and arbitrary pretensions with respect to America.

XIX. That the eight militia companies in the county, provide themselves with proper arms and accouterments, and hold themselves in readiness to execute the commands and directions of the General Congress of this province and this Committee.

XX. That the Committee appoint Colonel Thomas Polk, and Doctor Joseph Kenedy, to purchase 300 lb. of powder, 600 lb. of lead, 1,000 flints, for the use of the militia of this county, and deposit the same in such place as the Committee may hereafter direct.

Signed by order of the Committee.
Eph. Brevard,
Clerk of the Committee.

Contemporaries of the Revolution argued that the document predated the official version, being drawn up May 20, 1775, but claimed proof was lost when the document was burned in an 1800 house fire. According to the North Carolina Historical Commission, there is no official policy concerning the Resolves, which collectively were touted as the first step toward independence and referred to as the "Mecklenburg Declaration of Independence."

The Resolves were re-published in the Raleigh Register on April 30, 1819 and again in the June 5, 1819 edition of the Essex Register. Although claims regarding the validity have been vehemently argued through the decades, complete with sworn statements from several men said to be in attendance, the "Mecklenburg Declaration" remains as folklore reflecting the genuine historical patriotism of citizens of North Carolina.

There are a number of documented Scots-Irish among those listed as signers of the Mecklenburg "Declaration." Ezekial and Thomas Polk were sons of Robert Polk of Northern Ireland, who settled in Somerset County, Maryland in 1735. John McKnitt Alexander bore the middle name of his Scottish ancestor. Rev. Hezekiah Balch was a licensed preacher of the Everlasting Gospel by the Presbytery of Donegal in 1766. William Graham was Scots-Irish, as was John Flenniken, who arrived in Pennsylvania and later settled near Beattie's Ford on the Catawba River in North Carolina. Robert Irwin was an elder in the Presbyterian Church and served as a member of the Provincial Congress from Mecklenburg County in 1776. Mathew McClure was born in Ulster and settled near the site where Davidson's College was established. Neill Morrison was the son of James Morrison, who was among the many Morrisons who had emigrated from Northern Ireland and settled early near the Iredell – Rowan county line. Benjamin Patton was descended from Scottish Covenanters who moved to Ulster, then to America, where he settled in what is now Cabarrus County. John Queary was Scottish by way of Northern Ireland. David Reese owned extensive land on Coddle Creek in North Carolina and was born in Pennsylvania of Scots-Irish ancestry. John Davidson and William Davidson were among the earliest to settle in the North Carolina backcountry, and the Davidson's Creek settlement became the location of the Centre Presbyterian Congregation, established before 1755.

Five days after the "Mecklenburg Declaration," winds carried the British Ship *Cerberus* into the Boston Harbor. On board were three generals sent by the Crown to bring the colony back into order. General William Howe was the senior officer and in his company were Major-General Henry Clinton and General John Burgoyne.

The people of Boston watched from the rooftops and gathered along the hills near the shore as British troops rowed longboats from the ships to make their landing. The thunder of the fleet's cannons rolled across the water as a cover fire was directed on an area known as Copp's Hill. Nearby was Breed's Hill, where the colonists dug their hasty fortification. Behind that was Bunker Hill, the site of the British landing and where a thousand militiamen were dug in as reinforcements.

The British declared victory in the Battle of Bunker Hill, but it came at a tremendous expense. Casualties amounted to nearly forty percent of the total force – 226 killed and 828 wounded. The colonial losses were high as well, with more than four hundred militiamen either killed or injured.

George Washington was not the unanimous choice to head the Continental Army, nor was it a position he had campaigned to achieve. The army he inherited was more an assemblage of men than a disciplined fighting unit. There was little or no training among any of those initially under Washington's command at their encampment at Cambridge, near Boston.

Descriptions of the soldiers pointed out their "wretched" state of dress, and – owing to their lack of laundry facilities – the general filthiness of both the men and the camps. Most of the men had come from farms and were used to a diet consisting primarily of vegetables, and some were taken ill by the change to a meat-laden diet.

A traveler riding into camp would pass through a wide range of sights, few of which resembled anything military. Soldiers, to fend off the weather, had thrown up primitive huts constructed of scrap boards, or made tent-like shelters of cloth and stakes. Others tossed together dirt homes not unlike the sod and turf homes of the Lowland Scots. Others came better equipped. A group from Rhode Island brought proper English tents and was as well organized as the British in the arrangement of their campsite.

When the troops showed little improvement even after weeks of training, Washington determined to affect a gradual replacement of the unruly troops, with other recruits that could be brought in with a better understanding of what was expected of them. Discipline was renewed and a strict line was drawn between the officers and the enlisted men, with both sides expected to act according to their position, or take "forty or fifty lashes according to his crime."

Recruitment began in earnest in the summer of 1775, and by July, some three thousand men arrived from Pennsylvania, Maryland, and Virginia. Washington's affection for the Scots-Irish as fighters was already established and the frontiersmen formed the bulk of his troops in militia companies during the French and Indian campaigns. From the western edge of Virginia came a number of men who would later fight in Daniel Morgan's Virginia Rifle Brigade. By February, there were more than seventeen thousand men under Washington's command.

The British, meanwhile, had twelve thousand troops under General William Howe. His men had little to do, not enough to eat, and continued illnesses during the winter months in Boston, and as a result, morale was exceedingly low, and hopes for improvement were slim.

From the safety of his ship off the coast of Virginia, John Murray, the Earl of Dunmore, attempted to conduct business as usual with the House of Assembly meeting at Williamsburg. The burgesses responded by declaring that Dunmore, by his actions, had abdicated, leaving power with the Committee of Public Safety.

Dunmore retaliated against the colonists by gathering a collection of ships that could move up and down the coast, attacking settlements and plantations. Prisoners, including two women, were taken, tobacco crops were confiscated, and offers were made to Virginia slaves for their services. Dunmore promised freedom to any slave who would join his "Loyal Ethiopian" regiment. Enough of them were lured to service that, in December of 1775, an armed party of slaves and Loyalists attacked a militia force of more than nine hundred men under the command of Colonel William Woodford. Woodford's men came from the Virginia backcountry and were experienced fighters and experts with the long rifle.

The North Carolina governor had assured the British that Loyalists were to be found in great numbers in the province, and that the defense of the Crown's interests would be easily managed. There were many Highlanders among those recruited, but number of Loyalist recruits fell far short of the North Carolina Continentals who were already marching with regularity.

At Widow Moore's Creek, in one of the early battles of the Revolution in North Carolina, the colonial militia handily defeated their Loyalist neighbors, and the British determined that the use of local troops would be an insignificant addition to their own forces.

The beginning of the revolution put emigration to the colonies on hold for all practical purposes. Although there was an understanding at the time of the origins of the various groups, the terms Scotch-Irish and Scots-Irish was not used in contemporary descriptions. As an ethnic group, they were called Irish, although they were of Scottish ancestry. They no longer shared ideals or the culture of their lowland ancestors. They were a distinct and separate race of people who left for America before the revolution. Those who remained in Ulster were assimilated into the Irish culture, and when boatloads of new arrivals landed on American shores during the potato famines in the 1800s, those arrivals were simply - *Irish.*

CHAPTER NINE

The Year of the Sevens

Significant differences existed between troops originating in the established colonial towns and villages in the north and east, and those from the frontier and the backcountries of the provinces.

Patriotism was not an issue and bravery was found in both camps. Despite the confusion that reigned at Bunker Hill, even Burgoyne conceded the retreat "was no flight; was covered with bravery and even military skill."

Washington was authorized to raise a force of twenty thousand men, but he was successful in recruiting only about half that number. The Continental Congress had provided that for their three years of service, each recruit would be given a bounty of twenty dollars, one new set of clothes per year, and a one-hundred-acre land grant. However, pay was regularly delayed and some promised clothing never arrived.

On the other hand, provinces were offering as much as thirty dollars for a shorter period of service, and many colonists opted to stay closer to home and serve in the local militia companies.

Experience on the front lines may have favored those on the frontier as well, having already fought against raids on their homes.

Among George Washington's accounts and payrolls of the French and Indian campaigns are listings of recruits, their enlistment dates and places, and descriptions, many of whom were drawn from eastern locales, but also drawn from Ulster immigrants. Some Scottish listings may have been Ulstermen as well, since direct Scottish emigration to the colonies before the Revolution was comparatively small. [Appendix N]

Fourteen of the forty-four listed in Bell's Company are designated as Scottish, Scotch, or Irish. While that number is a large percentage, it may not reflect the total Scots-Irish in the company. Fourteen others are listed as English and two carry a Dutch designation. The remaining fourteen may have originated in Ulster as well.

The Size Roll of Mercer's Company includes similar percentages of Scotch-Irish from Tidewater counties such as Prince William and Prince George. Although features varied widely, the listing for Archibald Lockard is fairly typical of the Scotch/Irish/Scots-Irish on Mercer's roll:

> [Age] 23, 5'6", planter, Scotland, dark complexion, smooth face, short curled hair, speaks upon the brogue.

Perhaps the most significant of the differences of the colonial fighting men was their temperament. The traits that exiled the Scots-Irish to the frontier became sought after attributes in soldiers. Any earlier disaffection for their quick-tempered bravado was lost when the cause of freedom swept through the Provinces.

Accounts of the Scots-Irish in the Revolution range from those implying they single-handedly turned the tide, to those marginalized their participation. Regardless, it was agreed that the Scots-Irish were fighters. From the

Watauga and Yadkin River settlements in North Carolina to the Shenandoah Valley and backcountry of Virginia, there were no hardier men than the Scots-Irish.

Many recorded their signatures on official records at the courthouses with an X, living solitary lives on the frontier farm, but they were just as quickly and vehemently incensed by any real or imagined injustice. They possessed a brash temperament that prompted action regardless of the odds, and hardiness discovered in the kingdoms of Ulster. They exhibited bravery forged in regular battles at the front doors of their settlements on the frontiers of America. They were stubborn, fiercely independent, toughened by decades of hardships, and skilled in the use of their deadly long rifles.

The Scots-Irish were comfortable in the woods with nothing more than a pouch of dried corn for their meal. They were excellent hunters and when the corn was gone, wild game was plentiful and easily taken. They were at ease on the back of a "horse creature," as many of the Scots-Irish called their animals. The Revolution in the west was fought from behind the rocks and trees of the forests, and the majority of the Scots-Irish in America were children of the forests and farms.

Finally, the trade tools of the Eastern colonists were the specialized implements serving an urban community, while the primary tool on the frontier was almost certainly the long rifle. It provided food, sport, and protection.

Weapons were scarce in the colonies, and those owned in the north and east were invariably a version of the musket known in slang terms as "Brown Bess." The flintlock gun weighed fourteen pounds, and had a three-quarter-inch-wide barrel that was forty-four inches long. To fire Brown Bess, gunpowder was poured onto a shallow metal pan with a trailing fuse leading into the barrel. There, more powder was packed along with a wadding of paper, and a lead ball. The flintlock sparked the powder in the pan, which ignited the trail of powder into the barrel, and the resulting explosion fired the ball from the barrel.

There was little requirement for aiming the musket. Troops in a line waited until the enemy was close, then closed their eyes against the blast and prayed their shot would hit something or someone.

Colonists continued to use the British method of loading and firing the muskets for nearly two years after the hostilities began.

Loading the musket was dangerous in itself. If a powder horn was not closed, the "flash in the pan" could ignite the entire horn, burning the man with the gun as well as anyone nearby. Brown Bess had such recoil that some rested the stock against a tree, and there are accounts of injury and even death, when the kick of the gun hit a man's chest instead of his shoulder.

Before colonists began manufacturing their own replicas of the English Brown Bess, small arms were in such short supply that Benjamin Franklin suggested troops be outfitted with bows and arrows, or spears. At one point, militiamen were called out and ordered to bring with them shovels, axes, or scythes to serve as weapons. On the frontier, however, Brown Bess had long been a stranger with the introduction of a refined weapon. It was called the Pennsylvania long rifle, or as it became known in later years – the Kentucky rifle.

In the hands of the Scots-Irish, it was simply a "rifle gun." It was the same tool purchased at the trading camps at the beginning of the Great Philadelphia Wagon Road, as families set out for the frontier. Often, when wills were recorded, the "rifle gun" was among the first items listed in bequests to the older sons.

Ironically, in the hands of backwoods farmers were the finest weapons of the time. The difference was in the barrel design. While the Brown Bess had a smooth bore, the frontier gun had a spiraling groove – or rifled – barrel, thus, the name *rifle*. The groove spun the bullet as it was ejected, which gave it an accuracy far superior to the musket.

The design originated in Europe but it was the backwoods frontiersman who ingeniously wrapped the bullet with a swatch of greased linen, allowing the irregular size of the lead shot to perfectly match the barrel.

A lucky musket shot might hit a target at fifty yards, but the Pennsylvania rifle was commonly fired with deadly accuracy at distances approaching one hundred fifty yards. When a captured long rifle was sent back to England for demonstration, potential soldiers were so dismayed at seeing its accuracy, the recruiting effort suffered tremendously.

Meanwhile, a call for volunteers from the Virginia frontier brought so many men that contests were staged to determine the most accurate sharpshooters. At one hundred yards, the marksmen aimed at an outline of a nose, drawn on a piece of wood. It is often repeated that before fifty shots had been fired, competitors were aiming at the hole in the target's center.

The selected men marched nearly six hundred miles to the camp at Cambridge. Ninety-six troops under the command of Captain Daniel Morgan made the march in twenty-one days and upon their arrival were described as "remarkably stout and hardy men." Not one had fallen out of the long trek.

They were soldiers who wore leather shirts on their backs and moccasins on their feet, and the "rifle guns" they carried were such a part of their existence that named them with such monikers as "Sweet Lips" and "Hot Lead."

Their look was anything but that of an army. They were lacking uniforms and as a result, troops varied in appearance from location to location. Many of those fighting from the militia ranks were seasonal soldiers who had to return to the farms to harvest or plant. The fighting accommodated such practices. Though the Revolution lasted eight years, fighting was intermittent throughout that span and battles were located across a fairly wide geographic region. The British considered the appearance of the backwoods militia to be completely unmilitary, and were equally critical of their battle tactics.

The Scots-Irish and others who inhabited the frontier and served in the French and Indian campaigns had learned much from the Native American style of combat. The British generally considered the American tactics cowardly or unfair, and at odds with all the "proper" methods of waging a war.

The demeanor of the troops also presented occasional problems for General Washington. Since many of the soldiers under his command had joined from the same areas, many knew each other well. The temperament of the frontiersmen made it difficult to take orders from one of their neighbors. Conversely, the Scots-Irish were quick to watch out for the welfare of their own, even going so far as to surreptitiously free the occasional acquaintance being held under military guard for a breach of discipline or other misdemeanor.

Washington sent most of the Continental Army to New York, correctly anticipating a British landing at Long Island. Daniel Morgan's company was among those sent to fight in the North, where the major battles of the Revolution were centered for the next twenty-four months.

By the winter of 1777-78, Washington's troops were gathered at Valley Forge, twenty-two miles northwest of Philadelphia, and were haggard and nearly frozen from inadequate clothing. Washington reported to the Congress that some twenty-nine hundred men were "unfit for duty because they were bare foot and otherwise naked." As the winter months progressed, so did the number of men who were incapacitated by the cold.

Blankets were used as coats, five hundred horses starved to death, and the men were ravaged by smallpox and typhus. For a three-month period during the winter at Valley Forge, Congress left vacant the post of Quartermaster General and supplies to the army became virtually nonexistent. More than two thousand men died during the encampment over the Pennsylvania winter months that closed the year of the Bloody Sevens on the frontier.

For the Scots-Irish in closest proximity to the wilderness, there were daily reminders of the allure of Kentucky. There were groups of travelers passing regularly along the Wagon Road, heading for that point where a branch led to the Cumberland Gap, the closest break in the mountains for passage out of Virginia. Financial considerations were always a factor, and many who could not afford to purchase land in the quickly filling areas of Virginia looked to the wilderness of Kentucky.

In 1777, Benjamin Logan moved his wife and two sons to the safety of Harrodsburg, a larger settlement that offered greater protection. Boonesborough had already been under a three-day siege, although the attacking braves finally withdrew into the forest when they could not break through Boone's fort.

When Harrodsburg was attacked, Logan knew the safety of his own settlement was in jeopardy. He had only fifteen men with rifles to protect the women and children who had been brought back from Harrodsburg. No one was allowed to leave without guard, and lookouts kept a constant vigil for possible raiding parties. While in the company of a sentry on May 20, a number of the settlers were outside the walls when the attack finally came; the clap of flintlocks broke the morning stillness and shot pounded against the wooden fort.

John Kennedy tumbled back inside the walls with four wounds, William Hudson was killed immediately, and Burr Harrison dropped to the ground wounded and unable to move. The women scrambled to the safety of the fort, along with James Craig, who escaped injury.

Later, Logan dashed outside the gates to recover the bodies of Harrison and Hudson. Surprisingly, he found Harrison still alive, but he survived only a few days. Hudson and Harrison were both buried inside the stockade.

For days, a siege was maintained around Logan's Station, with occasional gunshots sounding against the timber walls. When the settlers returned the fire, time after time, and day after day, it became apparent that the supply of powder and shot would soon be exhausted. Logan took on the task of going for help.

In the dark of night, he slipped from the stockade, and made his way south through the forests, leaving Skaggs' Trace for the security of the deep woods on his way to the Holston Valley. He was gone for ten days, but returned with a pack full of supplies and word that men from the southern settlements had volunteered to give assistance. Two companies of militiamen eventually arrived, and the threat of attack was lessened.

In June, Guy Carleton sent word to Henry Hamilton, the lieutenant governor of Detroit, to enlist the aid of the native tribes in staging raiding parties and "employ them in making a Diversion and exciting an alarm upon the frontiers of Virginia and Pennsylvania." The frontier lands of Kentucky were considered a single county of Virginia at the time, and would be included in Carleton's order.

The first big raid was delayed several months, but it was of major consequence when it occurred. Daniel Boone and several companions were gathering salt at Blue Licks when he was captured by the Shawnee and was taken to one of their villages in Ohio. He was adopted by Chief Blackfish, and was taken to Detroit where the British questioned him about the strength of the forces in Kentucky.

When the chieftains and Boone returned to Ohio, he learned of a planned attack expedition through Kentucky. He managed to escape and return to Boonesborough. The ensuing attack lasted three weeks, and although the settlers successfully repelled each assault, food was running short and the water they had hoarded was nearly gone. Chief Blackfish, with plenty of powder and shot but unable to break through the walls and its defenses, decided to tunnel underneath. The settlers could hear the activity, and opted to dig their own tunnel at a right angle, hoping the Indians would break through and be caught defenseless.

When night fell, the roaring commenced, but instead of a powder explosion from a tunnel under the fort, it was the rumbling of a thunder from a storm that brought torrential rains. The next morning, the settlers looked outside at the tunnel; it had collapsed under the torrent of water. The enemy had vanished.

As the tribal warriors departed the Boonesborough stockade, they divided and went separate ways; one band was to strike Logan's station. Benjamin Logan was warned in advance of the attack and made extensive preparations for defense.

He stored supplies to carry residents through in the event of an extended siege. The settlers had a herd of cattle grazing about two miles from the Station, and Logan decided to bring as many inside the stockade as he could, and chose to run the risk alone. When he neared the herd, the Indian party spotted him and fired; Logan was hit and his arm was broken.

Severely wounded, he gave rein to his horse and galloped back to the fort, outpacing the pursuing warriors. While his wounds were dressed, Logan sent a messenger to the Holston Valley asking for reinforcements, and conferred with the men of the settlement on the need to hold out until help arrived.

Logan and his small community waited for three weeks for the attack that never came. When the men from Holston finally arrived, they were ready for a fight, and not finding one at Logan's Station, they traveled first to Boonesborough, then to Harrodsburg hoping to find support for a counterattack. After discussion, the men from the South agreed it was too late in the season to start anything, and they simply returned to their Valley.

The events that preceded the attack on Boonesborough and the attack that never materialized at Benjamin Logan's Station caused a major controversy on the frontier. There are differing opinions as to Benjamin Logan's position; some say he was upset with Daniel Boone and accused him of surrendering at Blue Licks and then consorting with the British at Detroit. Others said Logan was merely asked to sit in as part of a general court martial proceeding. Regardless, Colonel Richard Callaway, a one-time close friend of Boone's, viewed the frontiersman's actions as improper, and convinced Logan that a court martial should be convened at Logan's Station.

Boone was shocked at the charges leveled against him. Even though he successfully argued the reasons for his actions, and was acquitted of wrongdoing, he was unable to bear the thought of being accused by his companions. In addition, Rebecca and his children, believing he had been killed, had left Kentucky months before his return, heading back to North Carolina. When Boone left the tribunal at Logan's Station to retrieve his family, he also severed his ties with Boonesborough in disgust.

He later founded another settlement, Boone's Station, north of the Kentucky River, but there were a number of discrepancies among land warrants drawn by Boone, and settlers could not be sure of holding clear title to their land. As a result, he sold major portions of land he owned, raising $20,000. He collected $30,000 from friends and set out in 1780 for Richmond to settle the claims. On his way, he stopped at an inn at James City, Virginia, where a thief crept in and stole his saddlebags. There were friends who commiserated with Boone's unenviable position and forgave him any debt of repayment. Others, however, believed he pocketed the money. His reputation was severely damaged by the scandal.

CHAPTER TEN

Beyond the Cumberland Gap

Blossoms painted the springtime valley of western Virginia, and for many Scots-Irish it was the spring of a new adventure. Although the distance between the Shenandoah Valley and the Kentucky frontier was substantial and the geography rugged, trips between the two locations were being made with regularity.

John, Joseph, and Abraham Bowman, whose families were among the pioneers of the Bluegrass State, made several trips beginning in 1775 when they were located near Harrodsburg. Joseph Bowman also maintained his home on Cedar Creek and made several trips between the Valley and Kentucky in the years 1775, 1776, and 1777.

Each time families crossed through the western counties of Virginia, moving with wagons, possessions, and animals toward the Indian Road, a new urgency swept the Scots-Irish community. Kentucky land was already being surveyed and the best land would quickly be acquired by the first settlers.

The Virginia Legislature placed a one-year time limit on receiving lands associated with bounty grants for military service. The claimant, or his representatives, could present a certificate from Lord Dunmore or from the County Court where the military service had been performed. Between 1779 and 1783, the Commonwealth of Virginia issued more than 1,400 land bounty grants.

Families were leaving regularly and despite reports of new attacks on the frontier, migration only increased.

Wagons would be loaded with bags of flour, sacks of corn and salt. Bags of seed would be required to start their planting in Kentucky. Stores of gunpowder and lead would be stacked where they were readily accessible. There would be little room for trinkets, given the amount of required goods and the distance to be traveled.

Colonel James Knox was early to migrate. In 1775 he set out after Benjamin Logan and continued to the far reaches of the region before settling near the falls of the Ohio River. He was still traveling between the two locations, as many did, for supplies or business -- or both.

Often Knox served as 'officer in command' when making the trip with a large party of families. Like the Bowman brothers, Knox knew the territory along Boone's Trail and could advise travelers of the best course. As the summer months began to slip away to fall, thirty families joined to make the long haul to Kentucky with Colonel Abraham Bowman, who had decided to end his frequent trips to the frontier by making Kentucky his home.

Along the trail, horses would look like pack-mules. Light pieces of furniture would be strapped across the backs of some animals, while others bore leather saddlebags outfitted with straps that carried an assortment of farming tools. There were crude baskets made of thin hickory that could be balanced on the sides of some horses and in which could be stored any bed linens or clothing, and occasionally a small child or two. Tied behind the wagons were milk cows and the spare horses, and in the hand of each adult was a rifle or a pistol.

As they moved along the road from Harrisonburg to Staunton to Lexington, more and more families joined in, some hurriedly gathering their belongings to take advantage of the opportunity. There were men who joined by themselves -- single men, or those scouting a homestead for their families -- who took a position at the front or the rear of the caravan as guards.

After passing the Natural Bridge in Rockbridge County, and heading through Roanoke, they would have covered over a hundred miles only to remain hundreds of miles short of their destination. The scouts and guards at the head of the party would be spread thin as the caravan forded streams and rivers, leaving men at the water's edge to make sure that each wagon and pack animal successfully managed the crossing.

As they families moved deeper into the wilderness, the sounds of the forests would make sleep difficult for many. Wolves were said to howl relentlessly, the underbrush rustled with the movements of night creatures, and owls hooted throughout the dark hours.

Since native tribes were known to travel the trail, many believed the sounds were human-made and an indication of imminent ambush. It was uneasy time in the dark forests between the warm glow of the hearths of the Valley and the relative safety of the Kentucky forts. Sentries were posted at the outer edges of the caravan at night, and scouts slipped through the darkness looking for signs of trouble. In the morning, the men would return with their reports, and the day's travel was charted accordingly.

Caravans moved parallel to the Holston River from Marion to Abingdon, to the edge of Bristol, and then generally camped at the Block House. The house of Colonel John Anderson marked the end of the Great Road and the true start of Boone's Trail. Anderson was also from Augusta County, and had built the unusual house two years earlier. It was made of stacked logs with each successive trunk set slightly off-center so the house was wider at the roof than it was at the floor. The Block House not only attracted attention because of its looks, but also because of its location. It was a mandatory stop for groups of travelers on the frontier and was a point of reference that found its way into conversations, recollections, and diaries.

Beyond the Block House was Boone's Trail, a thin trace that would lead travelers across the Clinch River to the Cumberland Gap, and onward into Kentucky. After resting for the night, the families gathered their belongings and their courage, and set out for the frontier. From the Block House, the wagons could roll several abreast, allowing company and conversation between the drivers, but as the trail narrowed, wagons were forced to move single file.

All along Boone's Trail, the men would spot signs that offered proof they were not alone on the path. Sometimes it was heavy-footed tracks left by buffalo or animal carcasses left by wolves. Other times, there were indications Native tribes might be near, if only in small numbers. Generally, when the men suspected an ambush was possible, wagons were halted and gathered into a defensive position.

As they drew nearer the Cumberland Gap, as many as two-dozen men might be sent ahead to scout the rocky overhangs and high terrain surrounding the narrow passage. It was hoped the scouting party would be large enough to deter any thoughts of ambush, but small enough that they could quickly move along the ridge over the Gap.

Any caravan would be extremely vulnerable as it passed through the Cumberland Gap, even moving as quickly as possible, it would take time to navigate the entire group through the narrow mountain pass.

Once through the Cumberland, the remainder of the trip was of little consequence. The Cumberland River was forded, as was Stinking Creek and Rockcastle River. Big Laurel and Little Laurel were successfully crossed. With each river crossing, the caravan could stop on the far banks to camp for the night. Once the majority of the wagons had passed through the running water, men began chopping trees and dragging them along the edges of the camp. The branches were stripped for firewood and the trunks were stacked into a crude wall to serve as additional security; with the river at their backs and a wall of timbers in front of them, each of the travelers could feel somewhat more secure in lying down for the night.

At a place called Hazel Patch, a narrow path led away from Boone's Trail that created a fork in the road. The path leading to the northwest was Skaggs Trace, and men looking each direction for the first time could only imagine what might exist at the other end. Along Boone's Trail to the north, travelers would eventually reach Boonesborough. If they followed the lesser traveled, the wagons would pass through Crab Orchard and Logan's Station on their way to Harrodsburg.

New settlers searched for land that would serve well for their purposes. They needed a nearby water source, and enough ready accessible timber for building houses and outbuildings, but not so many that farming would be difficult. Elbow-room between the neighbors was also a prerequisite. Logan's settlement filled rapidly with the new families that were pouring into the Kentucky territory.

A single man good with an axe could build a small house in two week's time. Cabins became numerous along Dick's River, back toward Boone's Trail east of Logan's. Just beyond a fork in Carpenter's Creek, named for another pioneering family, was another thin trail that crossed from near the Kentucky River southward to the Green River Valley. The Huston brothers settled at a location called Hanging Fork, the site where exhausted and exasperated Virginia lawmen decided to enact frontier justice rather than continue to escort two unruly prisoners back home.

It was an appropriate time to be sizing up a homestead in Kentucky; in an effort to straighten out some of the problems with land surveys, the Virginia Land Commission planned hearings at Logan's Station, Louisville at the Falls of the Ohio, Boonesborough, Harrodsburg, and at Bryan's Station.

Raids on the settlers happened with regularity, and it was important to construct a structure sturdy enough to provide some security, and have construction completed as quickly as possible.

In the meantime, the wagons and the supplies were hidden in the nearby woods, and the horses tied nearby. If they felt threatened, frontiersmen in Lincoln County could take the horses and ride for the safety of nearby Carpenter's Station, or the added security of Logan's Station.

Since the logs were uneven and large gaps remained, river mud would be mixed with dried grasses to form a paste that would fill the gaps. Rocks would be collected and used to build a fireplace and chimney. Until a crude cabin was completed, families were forced to sleep outdoors or in what space could be arranged in a wagon.

In Kentucky, officials hoped to avoid some of the earlier disputes among frontier landowners. By 1780, settlers had pushed some fifty miles southwest of the first Kentucky settlement at Harrodsburg, into a then-forested region, with prairie grass valleys along the Green River.

In addition to the military bounties, there were tracts deeded to settlers who had "really and bona fide settled themselves" in the area by building cabins "upon any waste or unappropriated lands." The secondary tracts were up to 400 acres in size. After statehood, land in the valley sold for thirty dollars per one-hundred acres, and anyone living on unclaimed land could buy up to two hundred acres.

Benjamin Logan, whose settlement was the center of activity for many incoming families, was deeded 200 acres on a branch of the Kentucky River in 1775, but many of his early holdings were in the Hanging Fork/Dick's River area. In 1781 alone, Logan was deeded more than 5,600 acres along the Hanging Fork branch, St. Asaph's Spring Branch, and the Dick's River. Hugh Logan had 1,000 acres at Hanging Fork in 1781, while James Logan had 800. John Logan, another major Lincoln County landowner, was deeded his first 1,400 acres on Dick's River on April 12, 1781, just days before a similar grant to Nathaniel Logan.

William Montgomery – the father-in-law of Benjamin Logan – was one of the first settlers in the upper Green River Valley, claiming a 1,400 acre tract "over the Knobs" from Logan's Station. At the time of his settlement, he had seen no signs of Native Americans, and built his settlement without a stockade fortification, said to be a contributing factor in his death during an attack in 1781. John Montgomery was granted deeds that same year for land on Carpenter Creek and Dick's River, as was William before his death, along with his son William Junior. Thomas, John (Senior), and Joseph Montgomery were all listed on deeds by 1784.

Two highly visible pioneers owned land at or near the early Carpenter settlement. Isaac Shelby, the man who would be sworn in as Kentucky's first governor in 1792, and Colonel William Whitley, a fearless leader of men on the frontier both held land near Hanging Fork on the Dick's River. Shelby had five separate deeds originally issued to him that amounted to more than 1,900 acres on "Nob Lick Br. Hanging Fk. Dicks R."

Despite the impressive holdings, he later built a home northwest of present-day Stanford that he called "Traveler's Rest." Whitley's home, built east of Logan's Settlement, remains as an outstanding example of architecture and construction on the frontier. Whitley was deeded 400 acres along the creek that bore his name in 1780, and nearly 2,000 additional acres on Dick's River before 1787.

Henry Boughman was granted 400 acres on February 15, 1781, and another 1,000 acres on Dick's River was dated February 17. The Boughman family was among those carving out a homestead in the lush valley, becoming prominent as mill owners and businessmen over the next two centuries. A watercourse named for them, Boughman Creek, became the home of James Renffro in 1784 when he was deeded nearly 2000 acres there.

Map of Early Kentucky Settlements
Courtesy of State of Kentucky, Secretary of State Office

The Carpenters were a frontier family that arrived early enough that the creek came to be called for their settlement. Conrod Carpenter (referenced in many spelling variations of Conrad) had two separate deeds issued for land at Hanging Fork on Dick's River, one for 400 acres and another for 1,000 acres. Between 1781 and 1787, more than four thousand acres were added in separate deeds to Adam Carpenter, Coonrod Carpenter, George

Carpenter, and John Carpenter, all in Lincoln County, and all primarily in the Hanging Fork area.

By 1781, Nathan Huston had also established a separate deed for 150 acres on Dick's River, and in 1783 was deeded 250 acres in Lincoln County. Brothers John, Nathan, George, and Stephenson were all listed on deeds by 1784, from Rolling Fork on Salt River in Jefferson County, to Nelson County to the Green River in Lincoln. Brother George, who remained in Virginia, was named on the deed to a 923 1/2 acre tract on Scagg's Creek in 1784. By 1785, Stephenson Huston was listed on deeds totaling 1,600 acres.

Nathaniel Evans was a major landowner that began his holdings with deeds at Hanging Fork. His first four properties in early 1781 totaled more than 2,000 acres but his lands eventually extended from the Crossroads at Hanging Fork through Nelson and Fayette counties. Seventeen additional deeds granted Evans more than 10,000 acres.

Abraham Miller began with 1,000 acres at Hanging Fork in 1781, while Andrew Miller was deeded 100 acres nearby the same year. Alexander and John Miller also owned land in the Green River - Dick's River area by 1787.

Thomas Ammons was granted 200 acres at Hanging Fork in 1783. A year later, David Anderson had a 1,000 acre grant on the Green River, and in 1785 he was granted another 1,000 acres. Nearby, Richard C. Anderson received a grant for 9,000 acres. William Monger settled on Green River in 1784, the same year Alexander Montgomery received his deeds.

The Allen family was granted land when it was a part of Virginia called Fincastle County, although the grant named the location as Kentucky County. Hugh and James Allen had three thousand acres along Beargrass Creek and Salt River as early as 1774, and Thomas Allen found a spot along Hanging Fork in 1785.

John Bowles, sometimes spelled Bowls, settled on 400 acres along Dick's River in 1783, although a few years later, he became a major landowner in the Rockcastle Creek area with a grant of 6,751 acres in 1786. Squire Boone, Daniel's brother, had 400 acres issued to him in Lincoln County in 1786, near Silver Creek.

The Bowmans were among Kentucky's pioneer families; Joseph was deeded 837 acres on Cane Run in Lincoln County in 1781, while brother James owned land in the Green River area by 1786. John Bowman, along with Isaac Hite and Company, were speculating in land and were deeded 2,000 acres along Clark Run and Knob Lick Fork in Lincoln County on March 9, 1784, and another 1,000 on March 15 at Hanging Fork.

The Lee family, including Hancock and Willis, were among the first in the area of present-day Frankfort, founding a settlement in that area called Leestown. Hancock was deeded land on Elkhorn Creek in 1780 as was John Lee. Some of their many relations and namesakes migrated southward to settle the Dick's River (or Dix, as it is spelled in the early Kentucky deed book) valley at the same time. Thomas Lee had 500 acres on the Dix in March of 1781, while Jacob Lee had 375 acres Paint Lick Creek in Lincoln County that same year. William Fleming Lee was deeded 1,400 acres at the same time on Huston Fork in Bourbon County.

Brothers William and Henry are jointly listed on two deeds on the North Fork of Licking Creek in 1780, totaling 1,500 acres, where a third brother, Richard Lee, also settled. Before 1785, Richard acquired land on Rowling (Rolling) Fork, as did Samuel, Joseph, William, and Henry Lee.

William's son Richard H. Lee bought land in 1797. Henry Lee was deeded 4,000 acres on the Cumberland in 1788, while Charles Lee settled on a 4,000-acre tract on Woods Fork years earlier, in 1783. George Lee built a home at Hanging Fork by 1791. Ambrose Lee bought land by 1800, and later added to his holding when he acquired several tracts from the Montgomery brothers on Green River.

Thomas Gay originally settled in Fayette County around 1784, but was in the Hanging Fork area by 1790, and was among those of that name that had settled the Pastures in the early Virginia grants.

Richard Clark had 666 and 2/3 acres on the Green River in 1784, while Jesse Clark settled on the Dick's River and 500 acres in 1785. Other early landowners in the Hanging Fork area were William Moor (1783), Daniel and John McCormack (1781), John McGuire (1783), James McKenny (1781), John Patterson (1781), John Reins (1783), George Reynold (1781), Joseph Russell (1781), John Rutherford (1781), Zachariah Smith (1781), George Spears (1784), James Speed (1782), and John and Spencer Stone (1781, 1783).

Rough times awaited those who made it to the end of the Wilderness Road by that fall. It was bitterly cold during the winter of 1779-80, and it was not just a typical winter cold snap. An extended spell kept temperatures below zero day after day, week after week, and month after month. Those who suffered through it and survived would comment for years that that it was the coldest weather ever faced on the American continent.

As it turns out, it was not the coldest ever, but at the time, in the threat of armed attack, on the leading edge of the sometimes-lonely frontier, it may have made the frigid temperatures feel all the colder.

In the wilderness of Kentucky, those who had already arrived were struggling to survive, and many caught on the Wilderness Road would not make it past the Cumberland Gap.

From the middle of November 1779 to the end of February 1780, Kentucky was suspended in a brittle landscape of ice and snow. Sap froze in the trees and burst the trunks; creeks and streams were nothing more than thin ribbons of ice, and even the Kentucky River was frozen to a depth of more than two feet. Settlers melted snow for drinking water and cooking, but animals in the forest were not so fortunate; even many of the settler's horses and cattle froze to death.

Until the bitter weather settled in, each day seemed to bring more families through the Cumberland, but one Scots-Irishman wanted only to be back in Virginia.

Colonel William Fleming was the Chairman of the Virginia Land Commission, entrusted to sort out land claims. Not all the deeds met Virginia requirements.

Working with Fleming were Colonel Stephen Trigg, Edmund Lyne and James Barbour. The four commissioners met at Logan's Station, where they listened to a steady stream of claims and accusations regarding deeds to land on the frontier. In six months, Fleming and Company adjudicated 1,328 claims that involved over a million acres of land.

Fleming kept a meticulous journal detailing life at Logan's Station and the frontier in general, and noted the hardships facing new settlers during the particularly rough weather.

> The effects of the severe winter was now sensibly felt, the earth for so long a time being covered with snow and the water entirely froze, the Cane almost all kiled, the Hogs that were in the Country suffered greatly, being frozen to death, in their beds, the deer likewise not being able to get either water or food, were found dead in great numbers, tirkies dropt dead off their roosts and even the Buffalos died starved to death, the vast increase of people, near three thousand that came into this Country with the prodigious losses they had in their cattle and horses, on their Journey, and the severity of the winter after they got here killing such numbers, all contributed to

> raise the necessaries of life to a most extravagant price.

Many considered themselves fortunate just to be alive to struggle through the winter. The Davis family, trying to find land and complete the building of a structure before the weather worsened, may have let haste overcome their caution.

Stopping at Rockcastle River, they barely had time to stretch after the day's ride when they discovered the water was rising around them. Before they could gather themselves and their belongings back into the wagon, the family was surrounded by swirling water and marooned on a thin strip of land.

Davis hoped that with the help of several men he would be able to rescue his family and tried to swim for help, but the cold and savage river proved to be too much; he was swept downstream to his death. His wife and children, huddled together without a campfire, froze to death during the night.

Despite Fleming's note that frozen deer were found "in great numbers," meat was such a rarity during those winter months that it could scarcely be had at any price. Instead, settlers were forced to eat the horses that had died from the cold. Others brought the horses and cows inside the cabins to keep them alive. Sanitation was deplorable.

> The Spring at this place is below the Fort and fed by ponds above the Fort so that the whole dirt and filth...putrefied flesh, dead dogs, horse, cow, hog excrements and human odour all wash into the spring which with the Ashes and sweepings of filthy Cabbins, the dirtiness of the people, steeping skins to dress and washing every sort of dirty rags and cloths in the spring perfectly poisons the water and makes the most filthy nauseous potation of the water imaginable.

As would be expected, many settlers were suffering from frostbite and exposure, with the frigid temperatures affecting both the first arrived and the recent arrivals to Kentucky. Just to survive was a testament to the hardiness of the frontier families.

CHAPTER ELEVEN

Over the Mountain Boys

Springtime found the Scots-Irish in the Dix River Valley trying to turn the land into suitable farms and working to complete the structures of their cabins after the long winter.

When the freeze finally ended at the end of February, those who had been encamped at the various stations through the winter moved back to their settlements and began preparing their home sites. Vegetation was brought to life early by the subsequent – and welcome – mild weather, as though bursting forth from the long and oppressive freeze.

Farmers gambled on the early mild spell to plant seed and were rewarded. Corn was "half a leg high" by the middle of April. Peach trees planted by earlier settlers were already bearing fruit and apple trees placed in the ground long before the winter for spring transplanting had grown so quickly that some were too large to move.

While the winter had settlers in Kentucky cabin-bound, there were setbacks for the rebels against the British. The victories of Cornwallis at Charleston and Camden had families nervous all along the North Carolina frontier. South Carolina had fallen back to Cornwallis and the British.

Reports to Cornwallis indicated that Buford and his Virginia infantry were nearby, and the British commander believed a force dispatched immediately would net an easy victory. Serving under Cornwallis was just the man for the job; Banastre Tarleton, a furious, adrenaline-charged, fox-and-hound type officer with little time for regrets or second-guesses. His mounted British Legion and a detachment from the 17th Light Dragoons thundered off along the north-bound road, racing against time to overtake Buford before he could reach safety beyond the border.

Buford learned Tarleton's force was approaching, and on May 29 dug in to face the attack. He set a line at a place called the Waxhaw, along the border between North and South Carolina. Tarleton charged the rebels immediately. Buford realized his chances for victory were slim and reluctantly gave an order to surrender. The white flag was barely unfurled when Tarleton's men shot down its bearer. Discovering their surrender would not be accepted, the rebels scrambled for their lives.

A surgeon named Robert Brownfield witnessed the defeat at Waxhaw, and penned an account.

> Viewing this as an earnest of what they were to expect, [the Virginians took up their arms again] to sell their lives as dearly as possible; but before this was fully affected, Tarleton with his cruel myrmidons was in the midst of them, when commenced a scene of indiscriminate carnage, never surpassed by the ruthless atrocities of the most barbarous savages.
>
> The demand for quarters, seldom refused to a vanquished foe was at once found to be in vain. Not a man was spared... [Tarleton's dragoons]

> went over the ground plunging their bayonets into everyone that exhibited any signs of life, and in some instances, where several had fallen over the others, these monsters were seen to throw off on the point of the bayonet the uppermost, to come at those underneath.

Tarleton's massacre of Buford's Scots-Irish regiment at Waxhaw had a profound effect on the colonists, both the rebels and the Loyalists, called Tories. After witnessing the strength of the British army, and filled with new courage, Tories emerged from hiding to settle scores with those neighbors who had joined the rebellion.

On the other hand, the rebellious Whigs were bitter over Tarleton's treatment of Buford and his men. "Bloody Tarleton" was ominously hissed through clenched teeth and "Tarleton's Quarter" became synonymous with the merciless treatment of men. Between the Whig's anger and the newly inspired boldness of the Tories, riots broke out that included armed fighting among neighbors and some attacks that were nothing more than outright murders.

Two weeks after Buford's defeat at Waxhaw, the militia was called out in the southwestern part of North Carolina. Tarleton's massacre of the Continentals occurred just forty miles south of Charlotte, and the Scots-Irish settlers in Mecklenburg County began gathering. By June 3, there were nearly nine hundred men in the vicinity of the courthouse. General Rutherford ordered the men to be ready, expecting Cornwallis would eventually enter North Carolina.

One of the men marching northwest ahead of Cornwallis was a Tory by the name of John Moore who had grown up near the south fork of the Catawba River in North Carolina. He had joined the British army the year before, and on June 7 arrived at his father's home wearing a suit of regimentals and carrying a sword. He claimed to be an officer in the North Carolina Loyalists Regiment and called a meeting of Tories to prepare for the arrival of Cornwallis.

Rutherford learned of the Tory gathering at Ramsour's Mill, near the present-day site of Lincolnton, North Carolina, and ordered Colonel Francis Locke of Rowan and Major David Wilson of Mecklenburg County to raise as many men as possible to put down the gathering.

The two, with Major Joseph McDowell, and Captains Falls and Brandon, marched their men to a point sixteen miles from the Mill.

In the resulting battle, the two groups fought at close quarters, but having no bayonets and no time to reload, the men were forced to swing their fists and the stocks of their guns. By the time the Whigs finally realized they had the upper hand, the remaining Tories had fled.

Both the Whigs and the Tories who fought at Ramsour's Mill were sons of North Carolina. There was no physical distinction between them, and neither side had uniforms. The only badge of identification was found on the soldier's caps: the Tories stuck a sprig of pine in their caps, while the Whigs placed a piece of white paper on theirs. As the battle began to turn and the momentum began to shift, many of the Tories simply removed their identifying mark, and slipped in among the Whigs until they could safely flee the area.

Since many of the fallen lost their caps, and given that no return muster accounted for troops after the battle, the exact number lost by both sides is unknown.

At least seventy men from the Scots-Irish settlement in North Carolina lost their lives in the Battle at Ramsour's Mill with another two hundred wounded. In addition to Captain Falls who died at the outset of the battle, Captains Dobson, Smith, Bowan, and Armstrong were killed. [Appendix O]

Cornwallis entered Charlotte on September 20, 1780, and designated the town as his headquarters in the campaign to bring North Carolina back under the Crown.

A force of one hundred fifty militiamen hoped to slow his progress.

Tarleton's Legion to disperse the militia, and the skirmish at Charlotte was brief, but carried a stiff toll. Among the Mecklenburg men killed were Lieutenant George Locke and four privates; Major Graham and five privates were wounded. The British lost twelve men and had more than thirty wounded.

Cornwallis was in possession of Charlotte, but it was not a position of security. Rebel snipers regularly picked off the sentries who were stationed at the edge of his camp, and eventually Cornwallis ordered the digging of holes in which the guards could hide. Rebel assaults continued following the fashion of quick ambush and immediate disappearance into the woods.

Tarleton later wrote of the period of time spent among the Scots-Irish in Mecklenburg County:

> It was evident, and had been frequently mentioned to the King's officers, that the counties of Mecklenburg and Rohan (sic) were more hostile to England than any others in America. The vigilance and animosity of these surrounding districts checked the exertions of the well-affected, and totally destroyed all communication between the King's troops and loyalists in other parts of the province. No British commander could obtain any information in that position which would facilitate his designs, or guide his future conduct.

When the British sent men out to forage for food, they did so at personal risk. Residents were customarily paid for supplies that were taken by the British, but the Scots-Irish of Mecklenburg hid in the woods to fire at British companies as they approached. Express riders carrying information to and from Cornwallis were regularly ambushed at the outskirts of town.

There was a substantial skirmish between the rebel militia and the British at Polk's Mill, some two miles from Charlotte. The British troops located in Mecklenburg County were described as being in the middle of a hornet's nest, and the "Hornets" were greatly aroused.

When the county militias gathered across North Carolina and Virginia, the talk eventually turned to Patrick Ferguson. The British Major was in charge of a regiment of Loyalists headquartered at the Ninety-Six settlement in South Carolina. Ferguson was self-confident to the point of being cocky, the son of a Scots-Irish lawyer, and although physically small, he was extremely clever and accustomed to having his way.

Ferguson, after being ordered to Charlotte, left troops behind to guard Ninety-Six, assuming many loyal colonists would join his force as they marched north. Along the way, Ferguson rousted Whigs from their homes, plundered the valuables, and ordered the houses burned.

One of those burned out was coerced by Ferguson into traveling over the Blue Ridge Mountains to deliver a message to Colonel Isaac Shelby, camped at the point where the present-day states of Virginia, North Carolina, and Tennessee meet. The young militiaman related Ferguson's tactics and the threat that Shelby should surrender at once or Ferguson "would come over the mountains and put him to death, and burn his whole country."

Leaving half his force at Ninety-Six proved to be a military blunder on Ferguson's part. Of greater consequence was his threat against the lives and homes of the backwoods Scots-Irish.

Their survival on the frontier was a testament to their hardiness in facing adversity. When the young man delivered the message for Ferguson, Shelby and his men were not in the least intimidated – they just got angry.

The Scots-Irish temperament made it tough to turn away from a threat. As a group they predictably made immediate and undiplomatic responses to such actions. Knowing the Scots-Irish, Ferguson should have realized the mountain men would reach for rifles instead of white flags.

The 'Over the Mountain Boys' gathered shot, powder, and rations and stuffed them into saddlebags. News of the threat swept through settlements and armed men poured from the hills to "settle up" with Ferguson.

By September 20, 1780, their force numbered more than one thousand, including 400 militiamen under the command of Colonel William Campbell. At Gillespie's Gap, Colonel Benjamin Cleveland and 350 North Carolina volunteers joined the march toward the South Carolina.

As for Ferguson, there were no recruits to be found to increase the size of his force. Instead, those he encountered were "the most violent young rebels" as he later described them – "particularly the young ladies." A scout returned with bad news: perhaps three thousand of them waited just ahead.

The size of the force concerned Ferguson less than the attitude of the men he had already encountered. He realized he could be in trouble and sent several couriers back by separate routes to enlist aid. None of the riders reached Ninety-Six.

When Ferguson turned to meet his reinforcements, it was at a flat hill called King's Mountain, and he arranged his troops in a defensive position. The narrow hill was protected on one side by a rocky bluff and Ferguson believed he could easily defend from above.

Benjamin Campbell took 900 mounted men and another fifty lacking horses who promised to keep pace by trotting behind. Upon his arrival, Campbell found Ferguson's force vulnerable to the rebel style of combat which kept them hidden in the safety of the trees, firing at the exposed British force..

Ferguson tried to rally his troops even as they were succumbing to fire. Almost immediately, Ferguson was hit as well, and he had hardly hit the ground before his men began to surrender.

Amidst the confusion of the battle, some rebels were unaware of the surrender while others – still angry over Ferguson's threat – continued to fire, some in revenge for Buford's men at Waxhaw.

The brutality of the continued assault shocked even the militia commanders. The cease-fire came with some argument and considerable difficulty.

James Collins was sixteen years old when he climbed the side of King's Mountain behind Shelby, and later wrote of what he saw that day:

> The dead lay in heaps on all sides, while the groans of the wounded were heard in every direction. I could not help turning away from the scene before me, with horror, and though exulting in victory, could not refrain from shedding tears.

The nine hundred Scots-Irish backwoodsmen herded 716 remaining Loyalists down the mountain as prisoners. 225 had been killed and 163 were badly wounded. Shelby lost 28 men, with 62 wounded. Cornwallis, who had reached Charlotte just before the Battle of King's Mountain, panicked at the news and immediately withdrew his troops back into South Carolina.

The mountain men, having settled the score with the man who would make threats against them, lowered their rifles and returned to their horses, mounted up, and rode back to their homes in the hills.

CHAPTER TWELVE

Scots-Irish in Early Kentucky

Raids by and against the Native American nations in the Kentucky region were often reported. The Scots-Irish families in early-day Kentucky expected hardships and were regularly subjected to them. Homes were frequently raided and livestock was lost to natural predators as well as tribal attack.

The Treaty of Greenville in 1794 established yet another line between the settlers and the Native nations, but like all lines drawn by treaty, they were only respected until new settlers arrived.

When Thomas Feland and his many sons and daughters moved into the Hanging Fork area, they settled on a tract of land not far from the cabin of early Lincoln County settlers Stephenson Huston and his brother Nathan.

Nathan Huston was no stranger to those at the court sessions at Stanford, including Benjamin Logan, John Logan, Hugh McGary, and Stephen Trigg, who had been named as Justices of the Peace. The first county court was formed in January of 1781, and the following month

Benjamin Logan donated ten acres that could serve as a location for a courthouse.

William Montgomery settled with his father and brothers at the headwaters of Green River, about twelve miles from Benjamin Logan's fort. William the elder was Benjamin Logan's father in law, and four cabins were built in the same area for family members, including the families of William Sr. and William Montgomery Jr. -- the grandson of William the elder, John Montgomery, Thomas Montgomery, and Joseph Russell.

In March of 1780, four cabins of the Montgomery family were surrounded in the night, and the following morning, William Senior and a slave child were shot and killed when they stepped outside. One of Montgomery's daughters ran two miles to Pettit's Station where a messenger was sent to Benjamin Logan.

By the time Logan and his men arrived, John Montgomery had also been killed and the remaining family members taken captive. Joseph Russell managed to escape. Logan was able to track the captors and obtain a safe release of the Montgomery family.

Families moving to Kentucky continued to increase in number and in 1780, settlers petitioned the Virginia Assembly requesting that Kentucky County be divided into three smaller counties, to make it easier for the settlers to conduct business:

> The setled part of the County of Kentuckey is of Late grown so Extensive that in a time of pace it would be extremly inconvanient for your petitioners to attend at the Courthouse mutch more so at present when an invetorate War rages with unremited violance.

Twenty residents signed the petition, which was returned with a favorable ruling, dividing the single Kentucky County into the smaller counties of Lincoln,

Fayette, and Jefferson, with county seats at Harrodsburg, Lexington, and Louisville. By 1784, Nelson County was formed, followed shortly by the creation of Bourbon, Mercer, and Madison counties in 1785. Mason and Woodford were also created before end of the decade -- in 1788.

Hustonville Men and Boys on the Creek Bank, Late 1800's

Numbered: 1. Frank Lusk 2. Unknown 3. Doc Drye 4. Tom --- 5. O.S. Williams 6. Millard Allen 7. George Bradley 8. C. Brown 9. Smith Yowell 10. Sam Lusk 11. George Tucker 12. Les M. Reid 13. Gil Cowan 14. Theophilus Luke Carpenter 15. William Huffman 16. E.R. Pearce 17. Fred Peacock 18. Sid Adams 19. J.H. Hocker 20. Jim Yowell 21. Calvin Carpenter 22. George Hunn 23. John Goode 24. Cora May Goode 25. Unknown 26. Will Routt 27. J. Austin 28. Mose Cook 29. George Good 30. Boyd Weatherford 31. Billy Williams 32. --- Williams 33. Paul Drye 34. Unknown 35. --- Peacock 36. R. Givens 37. Luke Carpenter

Courtesy: Baughman Family

The petitions of the early day Kentucky residents to the Virginia Assembly are filled with the names of Scots-Irish, although the presence of the group as a separate, isolated community may have diminished with the lessening threat of attack. As communities became more populated, more stable, and – most importantly – more convenient, persons who "removed" to areas along the edge of the frontier became much more diverse.

Temperance Rally, February 1912, Hustonville Kentucky

Saloons and taverns became the focus of Temperance Societies that promoted demonstrations such as this one in front of the Newton Hotel in Hustonville. Building to the left: Corner of the National Bank - Rontenberg Store.

Courtesy: Baughman Family

The continued migration of families to the frontier was still a rigorous undertaking. Although traveling the wilderness was becoming easier, the system of trails constituted one of the primary problems facing the settlers -- they were still too primitive to even be called roads.

As cabins sprang up throughout the area, there were more complaints about the difficulty in getting from one place to another, particularly traveling to some of the larger settlements like Danville.

Several men were ordered by the court to survey the lands from Danville to the mouth of Hickman Creek, and report back to the court the best route for a road. At the same time, Stephen Huston, Isaac Shelby, Jacob Spears, Robert Barnett, William Reed and William Warren were asked to look at how a road might best be laid from

Danville to Widow Carpenter's land, on Carpenter's Creek.

Hustonville Christian College, circa 1900
Located at the present-day site of the Hustonville Elementary School, at Hustonville, Kentucky, the two girls marked by X are Sadie and Bessie Baughman; standing behind Sadie is Ada Cunningham Baughman.
Courtesy: Baughman Family

The court had reason to select the men they did, since the road would pass on, or near, the lands of the men doing the surveying. Several weeks later, Huston, Shelby, and Reed returned with their report, and the court ordered the establishment of a road to run from Carpenter's Creek near the plantation of Thomas Feland, passing near William Warren's house before heading in a line to Danville.

On February 16, 1785, John Cowan entered the Lincoln County court bearing a commission from the Governor that appointed him Sheriff of the county. Before moving to Kentucky, John Cowan had wed Mary Craig, the daughter of John and Sarah Craig who lived in the McGaheysville area of Rockingham County, VA, evidence of the migration of the Scots-Irish from western Virginia into central Kentucky.

Stephenson Huston Plantation House, Hustonville Kentucky
Built by Stephenson Huston on the Hanging Fork of Dick's River, the town of Hanging Fork, later called Hustonville, was settled between this and the identical home of Nathan Huston, built to the east in 1792.

It wasn't always the Sheriff Cowan receiving the initial notification when trouble arose. In Lincoln County, the man who lived at Sportsman Hill was often the first to know when events occurred, especially those on the Wilderness Road. Colonel William Whitley was a Scots-Irishmen who had come to Kentucky early, but had sacrificed a good part of his early land holdings to pay for the construction of a fine house between Logan's Station and Crab Orchard. No house like it existed on the frontier, and it remains as a legacy of early Kentucky craftsmen.

The red brick for the walls was carted in from Virginia, and are decorated with a series of lighter bricks forming a diamond pattern. Above the door, white bricks outline the initials of the home's owner -- W.W. -- and Whitley had his wife's initials inset on the opposite side. The ground floor windows are mounted particularly high as protection from attack. In addition, Whitley had a secret panel placed in a wall on the third floor where women and children at the house could hide in the event of an attack.

Log Outbuilding on Huston Plantation House
Originally a slave house and later a smoke house, this small cabin stood just east of the main house at the west edge of Hustonville Kentucky.

Whitley's home is believed to be the first brick house built in Kentucky, and served as the site of some lavish parties and barbecues for people of the county.

William Whitley had shown that it was possible to build a fine home, even at the edge of the frontier, when he completed construction of Sportsman Hill.

About the same time as Whitley's construction, Isaac Shelby completed his home, which he called "Traveler's Rest," about eight miles from present-day Hustonville. From his leadership in the Revolution and on the frontier,

Shelby had earned enough respect to be selected as Kentucky's first governor.

"Traveler's Rest" was a frontier home built of native stone outfitted to suit a man of position. On the first floor walls Shelby had waist-high paneling of polished cherry wood, and throughout the house woodwork consisted of fine cherry wood and walnut. The home later burned and a marker notes its original location.The Huston brothers employed the same builder for two homes at Hanging Fork, and features of Shelby's home were repeated in the Huston houses.

Exterior windows were high enough to discourage attack. The chimneys rose through the houses with fireplaces and hearths on both floors. A secret attic access could be reached by retractable ladder.

Nathan Huston constructed his home just over a mile east of his brother, and the two homes served as bookends for the small town that grew up between them. The house built at the east end was destroyed by fire, but the plantation house of Stephenson Huston survived more than two hundred years since its completion and was still standing at the end of the twentieth century.

Presbyterian Churches were no longer the only meeting places in extremely rural areas. As more families moved to the frontier areas of the country, intermarriages of faiths and nationalities became commonplace.

The Scots-Irish brogue became a wilderness colloquialism as children born along the frontier were exposed to other dialects, but some of the Ulster bloodlines remained intact well into the mid nineteenth century. As the country emerged from its infancy and the interactions of the populace were no longer limited to those living in immediate proximity to each other, the cultural separation of the Scots-Irish diminished.

CHAPTER THIRTEEN

Into the Nineteenth Century

Benjamin Logan was one of the instigators regarding statehood for Kentucky, and several conventions were held concerning the proposal. Those meetings were held in the summer of 1784, when Logan had heard rumors of a major assault on the Kentucky settlements by one of the tribes in the area. As a matter of caution, he called together as many of the influential men on the frontier to consider some measures for defense.

As it turned out, the rumors were false, but the meeting at Danville gave the men an opportunity to discuss among themselves the situation they were in, primarily the number of miles to the seat of government in Virginia, and steps that might be taken to secure protection for their families. Statehood for Kentucky had widespread appeal and a local government that understood the frontier ways might better serve the settlers.

Some twenty-five men gathered in Danville in December of 1784. They were men from each militia company, sent as representatives to a gathering that had no legal authority, but hoped to move toward that end.

While some of the men were eager to get on with the push for statehood, the items they proposed were inherently difficult. Attacks on the settlers had begun again, and few opportunities existed to discuss conventions. In addition, the proposal to publish an address to the citizenry required that the address be written by hand, since there was no printing press in all of Kentucky.

The men from the Dick's River valley were anxious to move forward. Riding from the area of present-day Stanford, Benjamin Logan, Nathan Huston, William Montgomery, and Willis Green hurried to meet Isaac Shelby at Traveler's Rest before heading on to Danville. Among the Lincoln County delegates was the man who would assume the responsibilities as the new state's first governor. [Appendix P]

Kentucky was admitted to the Union June 1, 1792, and Isaac Shelby was sworn in as the state's first governor four days later. Among the issues facing Shelby was the creation of suitable roads, a topic affecting the more than 70,000 people who were now living in the state.

The federal government had established a postal service in 1789 but the mail did not extend into Kentucky due to the rugged nature of the journey, and Shelby intended to improve the road from his farm near Danville through the Holston Valley and onward toward Virginia. The young state had no money, so Shelby began a private fund with a small contribution of his own.

John Logan and James Knox jointly supervised the road construction along the Wilderness Trail from Crab Orchard to the Cumberland Gap. Trees were trimmed or cut down, overgrowth was hacked away, and the trail was widened as the workers turned a path into a road.

As the road improved, the number of settlers increased dramatically, but where the earliest on the frontier were inclined to find shelter in stockades or forts, the post-Revolution wave of families built solitary cabins from stacked tree trunks.

The majority of the rustic cabins were heated in a single room, since stoves were non-existent on the early frontier and fires were maintained only in the main family room. Fireplaces came later, as did plaster walls constructed of straw and paste-mortar, applied to the interior of the walls. Paint came much later, and as a result, the houses of the settlers quickly took on a weather-beaten look and were replaced more often than refurbished.

Many of the farmers were also slave owners, and often when the farmer's family moved into a new house, the old house was outfitted for the slaves.

Those who left comfortable homes in the east might struggle mightily to achieve a comparable degree of comfort. Dirt floors were commonplace in the earliest cabins although some featured split logs called puncheons, lessening the mud but given to splinters from the unsanded surfaces.

Early settler William Poague built a loom by driving posts into the ground, which allowed cloth to be woven from flax or buffalo wool, and Ann McGinty brought her spinning wheel, which may have been the first on the Kentucky frontier. She used it to spin coarse linen from nettles. As a rule, the daily wear of the earliest frontier families was less than fashionable, and would remain so until long after the attacks on Kentucky settlements ended.

A postal route was finally established into Kentucky in August 1792, when Thomas Barbee of Danville was named the first postmaster. Delivery was not always as regular as the residents might have hoped, but each arrival was cause for excitement.

Mail delivery was eagerly announced at each town along the trail, since the riders not only carried correspondence, but also brought the latest news in a timelier fashion than ever before possible. People along the frontier were able to keep up with current events from the rest of the country, only days or weeks after they had occurred. Having ridden many miles between stops, riders were invited to rest at the local public houses and share the news and the company.

Inns along the road offered food, drink, and lodging to travelers, and although the custom of the time was to open the doors to strangers who needed to stop for the night, the risks involved with that practice on the frontier reduced the number of willing hosts. One of the indicators was found on the door itself; a rope or heavy cord was threaded through an opening, which – when pulled from the outside – would lift the interior latch, allowing the door to open. To keep people out, the door was effectively locked by simply drawing the cord back in through the opening. Inns and "rooms" were able to create a profitable enterprise for the owners who kept the latchstring out for travelers.

The arrival of a horse was generally noticed inside the house, but if the door remained closed, the rider would call out a request for accommodations. "Get down and rest your saddle," was a common reply to such requests, even if there were no longer spare beds. The beds and straw beds went to the early arrivals, leaving the latecomers to sleep on the floor, which was still preferable to sleeping outdoors.

On Christmas Day in 1797, a posse led by Capt. Joseph Ballenger arrived at Hanging Fork and arrested two men and three women, described as heavily tanned and between twenty and thirty years of age. The leader was a big man with dark, curly hair and heavy eyebrows. The other man had red, curly hair and was slightly smaller in size. All three women were pregnant and the entire group's clothing amounted to little more than rags.

When asked, the men replied that they were brothers – Micajah and Wiley Roberts – and reported that the women were sisters. Susanna and Sally Roberts were said to be the wives of the two men, and the third woman was identified as Betsy Walker. Ballenger bound all five at the wrists for the trip from Hanging Fork back to the jail at Stanford, where the men were wanted for murder and robbery. The body of Thomas Langford had been found hidden under a pile of brush and leaves.

The two suspects were later identified as the infamous Big and Little Harpe, whose escapades in North Carolina were the talk of the frontier, their actions quite possibly those of the first serial killers on the American continent. They were sons of a Tory farmer and had terrorized the countryside with their robberies, horse thefts, ambushes, and murders. Numerous assaults on the Wilderness Road were also attributed to them. On March 16, 1798, ten days after the second woman gave birth in jail, the brothers managed to escape their chains and overpower a jailer.

The Harpe brothers left the women and their babies behind, and as time passed, Danville residents softened their positions concerning the women housed in their jail. The Harpe women claimed innocence in their husbands' activities and residents took up a collection, bought clothes, found a donated horse, and outfitted them with enough supplies to get them back to their home.

Once the women reached Crab Orchard, however, they slipped off onto a rarely traveled trail, made their way to the Green River, and traded the mare for a boat. The three women and their infants paddled more than seventy miles along the Green and Ohio rivers until they reached a place called Cave-in-Rock, where river pirates and desperadoes kept out of the reach of the law.

There, they were reunited with Big and Little Harpe. The women might have regretted the move; the infants proved to be a difficult addition to the movements of the wanted men, and in a fit of rage, Big Harpe murdered Betsy's daughter.

One of the largest and wildest manhunts in early-day Kentucky ensued before Big Harpe was finally tracked down and killed. His head was placed on top of a trimmed sapling in Hopkins County, Kentucky, and the skull remained as a grim reminder long enough for the spot to be called "Harpe's Head."

Little Harpe's fate, although less grisly, was similar to his brother's. He moved from Kentucky to Mississippi territory, where he continued living the life of an outlaw until he was finally caught and executed.

The death of Big Harpe came on July 22, 1799 – and by that time the young state featured advances of both large and small scale. A newspaper began publication and a line of packet boats began making trips from Pittsburgh to Cincinnati with regular stops at Maysville, Kentucky. Less importantly, the legislature passed an act in 1795 that required each white male over sixteen years of age to kill a certain number of crows and squirrels every year.

The Scots-Irish continued their interest in public office and public education with new ventures in Kentucky. The Scots-Irish Presbyterians of Lincoln County established the first chartered school in Kentucky. Reverend David Rice applied for and received a charter to conduct a school in his home in Danville under the name of Transylvania Seminary. It was later moved to Lexington and removed from the auspices of the Presbyterians, which prompted church leaders to solicit some $10,000 in endowments, including contributions from President George Washington and Vice-president John Adams to establish Kentucky Academy.

The new nation was of considerable interest on foreign shores, and numerous correspondents reported from the frontier. J.P.B. de Warville roamed the countryside beginning in 1788, and in his writings about those in Kentucky he noted separately the Scotch and Irish, although there was little direct immigration at the time by any group other than the Scots-Irish.

The national features here are not strong...we still see the liberal English, the ostentatious Scotch, the warm-hearted Irish, the penurious Dutch, the proud Germans, the solemn Spaniard, the gaudy Italian, and the profligate French...

I have just returned from a tour of ten days into the interior of Kentucky... thickly settled with excellent well built farm houses, and raising wheat and corn. I mounted my horse and continued the road to Lexington... a mere buffalo track, following skillfully the ridges of hills and mountains. Lexington is composed of upwards of three hundred houses ranged into streets intersecting each other at right angles. They are built principally of brick. The public buildings consist of a University, Court-house, market, Hall, Bank, and four Churches... one Lutheran, one Presbyterian, and two sects of Methodists. The inhabitants shew demonstrations of civilization; but at particular times, on Sundays and market-days, they give a loose to their dispositions, and exhibit many traits that should exclusively belong to untutored savages...

I found the country exceedingly well-timbered... numerous farms chequered this rich scene, producing wheat, corn, oats, flax, hemp, tobacco, cotton, and vegetables of all kinds... I stopped at the house of a cultivator... a log one, fitted up very well... the dinner consisted of a large piece of salt bacon, a dish of homslie, and a turreen of squirrel broth... the Kentuckyan ate nothing but bacon, which indeed is the favourite diet of all the inhabitants of this State, and drank nothing but whiskey.

By the turn of the century, the population in the valley of Dick's River and Carpenter Creek had increased immensely, as had the towns of Stanford and Danville.

The population of Lincoln County, Kentucky by 1810 was a mix of pioneer families, primarily from western Pennsylvania and the Scots-Irish settlement in Virginia. There is no simple method for determining the origin of that populace, and the results of any study can be disputed.

Understanding that last names can be traced to specific regions allows for conjecture. However, the original Ulster colonization consisted of Scots and English who intermarried and, by the first migration to America, were ethnically independent of the Scots, Irish, and English. The lowland Scots largely bore names based in Middle English and Old English rather than Gaelic. Spelling was not standardized until much later, and literacy was not as widespread as in later years, allowing for spelling variations by both family members and those recording the names. Additionally, some of the handwritten records are difficult to decipher.

Comparison of the 1810 US Census for Lincoln County with known Scots-Irish lists and references indicates a sizable percentage of Scots-Irish. Allowing assumption (for example, Diar as a respelling of Dyer), 289 of the 937 named heads of households, or 30.8%, are names found in a listing of lowland Scots recorded in the first half of the 16th Century. The Aberdeen Registry, as an incomplete census of the lowlands, lowers the resulting percentage from what it might have been.

Additionally there are Scottish names not included in the Aberdeen Registry that are known Scots-Irish in Kentucky. The simple inclusion of those names beginning with the Scottish patronymic indicator *Mc* and a conservative addition of known Ulster Scot names brings the percentage of Scots-Irish to 35.8% of the 1810 Lincoln population.

Additionally, there are 673 surnames listed in the so-called Scotch-Irish Settlement in Virginia that appear in the 1810 Lincoln County, Kentucky census, or 71.8% of the population. Even a median figure between the high and low estimates places the number of Scots-Irish at over 50% of the population.

By the mid-1800's, when the wave of true Irish immigrants began to appear in the United States, the Scots-Irish might still be distinguished by their speech or their temperament, but in general, they had been on the continent for a century, and many families who comprised the earliest of the Great Migration waves from the North of Ireland had been in America nearly 150 years. They were regarded as long-time neighbors, the sons and daughters of pioneers, and contributing citizens in the American Society. When the Irish potato famine brought boatload after boatload of impoverished Irish to American shores, those who had come earlier from the North of Ireland began pointing out that they were Scottish "by way of Ireland" – or Scotch-Irish – and not to be confused with those recently arrived.

ACKNOWLEDGEMENTS

Thanks to all responding to email questions, including the many library and reference desk staffers across the country.

I owe a debt of gratitude to all those who made suggestions and offered research advice, including the library staff at the Tulsa City-County Library, and those at Cass County (MO), Casey County (KY), Lexington (KY), Stanford (KY), Latter Day Saints FHC (Tulsa), Sapulpa (OK), Staunton (VA), and Salisbury (NC).

Also, those staff members at governmental agencies who were most helpful, including Augusta County (VA) Clerk, Cass County (MO) Historical Society, Genealogical Society of Rowan County (NC), Harrison-Rockingham Historical Society (VA), Holt County (MO) Recorder, Kentucky Genealogical Society, Lincoln County (KY) Clerk, the University of Kentucky, and the North Carolina State Archives.

Additionally, my appreciation for assistance above and beyond by the late Katherine G. Bushman of Staunton, VA; the late Maxine Heidrich of Cass County, MO; Barbara Lowrey, Kathy Huber, Betty Black, Sam and Margaret Baughman, Madeline Hilbert of Dayton, VA; James Kluttz of Landis, NC; Mr. and Mrs. Gary Lynn of Hustonville, KY; Evelyn Stallings of Salisbury, NC; Gaither Shrumm of Lincolnton, NC; Lucille Ullery of Freeman, MO, and the many others whose names should be included, as well as those whose patience and encouragement served so well; and a special and sincere thanks to Martha Lee Huston Hoefling, as well has her daughters Linda and Kathy, who have always been there with a word of encouragement when it was most needed.

Appendices

Appendix A

Lancaster County, PA Deedholders.

Early to depart the Ulster Plantation were immigrants named Allen, Allison, Anderson, Bailey, Baston, Bayley, Beach, Bealey, Black, Blazer, Bringham, Brown, Brownlow, Bryan, Buchanan, Buey, Campbell, Clark, Cloud, Cook, Couch, Cunningham, Davison, Doaks, Dunning, Galbraith, Gardner, Gay, Guy, Hairston, Hamilton, Harris, Houston, Howard, Huston, Hutchinson, Inless, Kelley, Kyle, Lowrey, Maris, Mayfort, McClung, McDonald, McFarland, McGinnis, McKee, Middleton, Mitchell, Monday, Moore, Scott, Smith, Sterret, Stewart, Taylor, Walker, White, Wilkins, Wilson, Wood, and Work.

Appendix B

Early Deeded Landholders, Donegal Region, Lancaster County, PA

1716: Robert Middleton

1717: John Stewart and George Stewart

1718: Peter Allen, Robert Buchanan and William Buchanan, William Bryan, Thomas Bayley, Henry Bealey, James Galbraith and John Galbraith, John Gardner, James Mitchell, Samuel Smith, John Sterret, Robert, Thomas, William Wilkins and John Wilkins

1720: Patrick Campbell, James Cunningham, Joseph Cloud, James Couch, Daniel Clark, Widow Dunning, John Mitchell, Thomas Mitchell, Ephraim Moore, James Smith, and Joseph Work

1721: John Taylor

1722: Robert Allison, James Allison, John Allison, Gordon Howard, Thomas Howard, Alexander Hutchison, William Maybee, Richard McFarland, Robert Monday, John Maris, James Kyle, and Hugh White

1723: John Miller

1724: Thomas Black, William Beach, John Black, Robert Brown, John Davison, John Doaks, Christian Gardner, John Walker and Michael Wood

1725: Jeremiah Bringham, Matthias Blazer, James Brownlow, Abraham Inless, Hugh Scott

1726: Rev. James Anderson, Joseph Baston, James Harris, Alexander McKee, George Mayfort

1729: Lazarus Lowrey, James Lowrey, John Lowrey, Daniel Lowrey, and Alexander Lowrey

1730: James Buey, James Cook, Peter Hairston, James Hutchison, John Kelley, William Mitchell, Alexander Mitchell, Thomas Scott, and John Scott

Appendix C

Anson NC Early Settlers

Conococheague Creek Settlers
John Beard, John Black, John Harris, David Houston, William McDowell.

Yellow Breeches Creek Settlers
Francis Beatty, James Crawford, John Morgan, Morgan Morgan, John McWhorter, John Rankin, William Robinson.

Conodoguinet Creek Settlers
James Cathey, Alexander Cathey, Archibald Cathey, Isaac Davenport, William Docharty, James Forster, John Potts, John Hunter, John Jones, John Lawrence, William Ralston, Rev. John Thompson.

Appendix D

Documented Early Settlers: Rowan Co. NC Scots-Irish Tract

Aaronhart, George
Aaronhart, John
Adams, John
Agenda, John
Agender, John
Agoner, Henry Sr
Agoner, Henry Jr
Ainsley, Alexander
Albright, John
Albright, Michael
Alexander, Evan
Alexander, James
Alexander, William
Allen, Bartley
Allison, Andrew
Allison, James
Allison, Mary
Allison, Thomas
Anderson, David
Anderson, Isaac
Anderson, James
Anderson, Richard
Anderson, Samuel
Anderson, William
Andrew, James
Andrews, James
Arand, Jacob
Armstrong, Abel
Armstrong, Mary
Armstrong, Richard
Armstrong, Robert
Armstrong, Samuel
Armstrong, William
Arndt, Godfrey
Aron, Peter
Aronhart, Phillip
Arrant, Conrad
Baker, A
Baker, Absolom
Baker, Benjamin
Baker, Christopher
Baker, Elizabeth
Baker, John,
Baker, John Jr
Baker, Joseph
Baley, Charles
Barne, John
Barbarick, Christian
Barber, Elias
Barber, Jonathin
Barber, Luke
Barber, William
Barkley, Henry
Barkley, Robert
Barkley, Samuel
Barr, Hugh
Barr, John
Barr, Patrick
Barr, William
Barringer, J
Barringer, Paul
Barringer, Peter
Bartley, John
Bashford, Thomas
Basinger, George
Basinger, John
Beam, Jacob
Beam, John
Bear, Henry
Beard, John
Beard, John L.
Beard, Lewis
Beard, M.A.
Beard, Valentine
Beaty, Charles

Beaty, Francis
Beaty, Thomas
Beaver, Daniel
Beaver, David
Beaver, Michael
Beaver, Nicholas
Beaver, Paul
Beaver, Peter
Beefle, Martin
Bell, Robert
Bell, Thomas
Bellah, Moses
Berger, George H.
Berger, Michael
Best, John
Betts, Andrew
Bettz, Andrew
Bettz, George,
Biles, Charles
Biles, Joseph
Biles, Thomas
Bird, John
Bird, Michael
Blackwelder, John
Blake, Hugh
Blake, John
Blue, Malcomb
Blythe, James
Blythe, Samuel
Bonachom, Michael
Boone, Jonathan
Bostian, Andrew
Bostian, Andrew Sr
Bostian, Jacob
Bostian, Jonas
Bostian, Methais
Boston, Michael
Bowman, James
Bowman, William
Brady, John
Braley, John
Braley, Thomas
Braley, William
Brandon, Alexander
Brandon, James
Brandon, John
Brandon, Richard
Brandon, Thomas
Brandon, William
Brazill, William
Brazle, William
Brem, Conrad
Bringle, Nicholas
Broner, Henry
Brougher, Jacob
Brown, Abraham
Brown, Andrew
Brown, Elisha
Brown, Henry
Brown, Jacob
Brown, John
Brown, Jonas
Brown, Leonard
Brown, Michael
Brown, Michael Sr
Brown, Peter
Brown, Samuel
Brown, Thomas
Brown, Timothy Sr
Brown, William
Bruner, George
Bruner, Phillip
Brunner, George
Bryan, John
Buck, Charles
Buckannon, James
Buis, Henry
Bullen, Conrad
Bullen, George
Bullen, John
Bullen, Phillip
Bullin, John
Buntin, James
Buntin, John
Buntin, Robert
Buntine, James
Buntine, John
Buntine, Robert
Buris, Edward
Burrage, John
Burns, John
Burrage, Edward
Burrage, George
Burroughs, Townsend
Butler, Adam
Butler, Harmon
Butner, David
Buyers, Richard
Caldwell, David
Callaway, Joseph
Campbell, John
Campbell, Joseph
Campbell, Matthew
Campbell, Patrick
Carlisle, Robert
Carn, Conrad
Carr, Andrew
Carruth, Adam
Carruth, James
Carruth, Robert
Carruth, Walter
Carson, Henry
Carson, James
Carson, John
Carson, Thomas
Carson, William L.
Carter, James
Casper, Adam
Casper, Peter
Caster, Jacob
Caster, John
Cathey, Alexander
Cathey, Andrew
Cathey, George
Cathey, Hugh
Cathey, James
Cathey, Jane
Cathey, John
Cathey, William
Cauble, Peter
Cever, Jacob
Chambers, David
Chambers, Henry
Chambers, Joseph
Chambers, Maxwell

Christman, John
Chunn, Thomas
Clary, Daniel
Clary, David
Clary, John
Clary, Sarah
C1ingman, Alexander
Cluts, David
Clutz, Jacob
Clutz, Jacob, Sr.
Cobble, John
Coble, Adam
Coble, Michael
Coble, Peter
Cochran, Andrew
Cochran, James
Cochran, John
Cochran, Robert
Cohen, John
Coldiron, Conrad
Coldiron, George
Coleman, Jacob
Coles, WilliamT
Collins, James
Collins, Thomas
Cook, Alexander
Cook. Thomas
Cooke, Alexander
Cooke, James
Coon, Antony
Cooper, Samuel
Copple, Peter
Correll, Jacob
Correll, John
Correll, John A.
Correll, Peter
Correll, Phillip
Corriher, Daniel
Cosby, William
Coughenour, Christian
Coughenour, John
Coughman, Leonard
Cowan, Benjamin
Cowan, David
Cowan, Henry
Cowan, Isaac
Cowan, John
Cowan, Robert
Cowan, Thomas
Cowan, William
Cowan, William Jr.
Cowan, William Sr
Craig, David
Craig, James
Craig, John
Craiglow, William
Crawford, Jacob
Creglon, William
Criter, Leonard
Croos, Phillip
Crowell, Teater
Cruse, Phillip
Culbertson, John
Culbertson, Samuel
Culp, Adam
Culp, Henry
Cummings, Michael
Cunningham, Humphrey
Daniels, James
Darr, Valentine
Davenport, William
Davis, George
Davis, Edward
Davis, Jesse
Davis, Richard
Dawsey, Patience
Deacon, James
Deal, Jacob
Deal, Joseph
Derr, Valentine
Dickey, James
Dickey, James Jr.
Dickey, Thomas
Dickie, Elizabeth
Dickie, John
Dickie, Thomas
Dickson, Joseph
Dillon, Jacob
Dillon, Michael
Dillon, Peter
Dixon, Michael
Dobbin, Alexander
Dobbin, Hugh
Dobbin, James
Dobbin, John
Dobbins, Alexander
Dobbins, James
Dobbins, John
Donaldson, Alexander
Donaldson, Andrew
Donaldson, John
Douglas, Thomas
Duff, George
Duke, John
Dunn, Barnabus
Dunn, Charles
Dunn, John
Dunn, John Jr.
Durham, Benejh
Eagle, George Jr.
Eagle, George Sr.
Eagle, John
Eagle, Phillip
Earnhart, Elias
Earnhart, George
Earnhart, John
Earnhart, Moses
Earnhart, Phillip
Earonhart, George
Earry, Peter
Eary, Abraham
Eary, John
Eary, Zachariah
Eddleman, Peter Sr.
Eddleman, Peter
Eller, Christian
Eller, Jacob
Elliott, John
Ellis, Radford
Enos, William
Ervin, Arthur
Ervin, George
Ervin, Joseph
Ervin, William

Erwin, Thomas
Fanning, Edmond
Felhower, Nicholas
Fennell, Frederick
Fennell, John
Ferguson, Andrew
Ferguson, John
Ferrand, Stephen L.
Ferrned, S. L.
File, Jacob
Fillhower, Nicholas
Fisher, Charles
Fisher, Fred
Fisher, Frederick
Fisher, George
Fisher, Hannon
Fisher, Jacob
Fisher, John
Fisk, Methias
Fite, Peter
Fitspatrick, James
Fitspatrick, Edmond
Fleming, George
Fleming, Robert N.
Forster, Hugh
Fost, Peter
Foster, David
Foster, Joseph
Foster, Owen
Foster, Samuel
Fraley, David
Fraley, George
Fraley, Henry
Fraley, Jacob
Frazier, James
Frees, Adam
Freeze, Jacob
Freeze, John
Freeze, Peter
Frick, Henry
Frick, Jacob
Frisal, Lydia
Frock, Conrad
Frohock, Alexander
Frohock, John
Frohock, Thomas
Frohock, William
Fullenwider, Henry
Fullenwider, Jacob
Fullenwider, John
Fullerton, David
Fullerton, William
Fulton, John
Gaither, Nicholas
Galbreath, Samuel
Galbreath, Thomas
Gallagher, Hugh
Gardner, David
Gardner, Francis
Gardner, John
Gardner, Matthew
Gardner, Robert
Garner, John
Garner, Mathias
Gates, Edward
Gheen. Thomas
Gibson, George
Gibson, James
Gibson, John
Gibson, William
Giles, Henry
Giles, John
Gilihan, Abraham
Gillespie, Elizabeth
Gillespie, Isaac
Gillespie, James
Gillespie, John
Gillespie, Matthew
Gillespie, Robert
Gillespie, Thomas
Gillian, Abraham
Gillispie, Matthew
Goodman, Christopher
Goodman, George
Goodman, John
Goos, John
Gottle, Peter
Graham, Fergus
Graham, James
Graham, John
Graham, Joseph
Graham, Moses
Graham, Richard
Grant, William
Gray, James
Gray, Robert
Gray, William
Greenfield, Thomas
Greeson, Nicholas
Grimes, Richard
Grimminger, Frederick
Grubb, Conrad
Grubb, George
Grubb, Henry
Guffy, John
Haggins, John
Hair,Thomas
Hall, John
Hall, Joseph
Hamilton, Archibald
Hamilton, Malcolm
Hamilton, Sarah
Hampton, William
Hanley, Darby
Harden, Robert
Hardy, Robert
Hare, Daniel
Harkey, Jacob
Harkey, Reuben
Harris, James
Harris, Robert
Hart, James
Hart, Samuel
Hart, William
Hartline, George
Hartline, Peter
Hartman, Charles
Hartman, Harmon
Hartman, John
Hartman, Michael
Hartman, Harvey
Hartman, John
Hartman, Robert
Hayes, David
Hays, James

Hays, Joseph
Hearne, James
Heathman, Hezekiah
Heathman, James
Heathman, Jonathan
Heilig, Henry
Heilig, Michael
Heitman, George
Hellard, George
Hemphill, James
Hemphill, Samuel
Henderson, Archibald
Henderson, Thomas
Hendrix, James
Hess, John
Hickman, Joseph
Higgins, John
Hileman, John
Hill, Abraham
Hill, Edward
Hill, George Henry
Hill, James
Hill, Reuben
Hill, Seth
Hill, Thomas
Hillard, George
Hillis, Robert
Hillis, Samuel
Hinds, Ralph
Hodge, George
Hodge, Jesse
Hodge, John
Hodge, Joseph
Hoffman, Francis
Hoffner, George
Hoffner, Henry
Hoffner, John
Hoffner, Leonard
Hoffner, Martin
Holley, Zachariah
Hollobough, George
Holmes, Moses
Holmes, Moses L.
Holmes, Reuben
Holms, John
Holshouser, Andrew
Holshouser, Jacob
Holshouser, Michael
Honberger, Valentine
Horah, Henry
Horah, Hugh
Horah, Margaret
Houston, David
Houston, James
Howard, Benjamin
Howard, Gideon
Howard, John
Hudson, John
Hudson, Thomas
Huey, Henry
Huggins, James
Huggins, John
Huggins, Robert
Hughes, Alexander
Hughes, Joseph
Hughey, Henry
Hughey, Henry S.
Hughey, Isaac.
Hughey, Samuel
Hughs, Alexander
Hughs, Hudson
Hughs, James
Hughs, Joseph
Huie, James
Hunt, James
Hunt, John
Huston, Agnes
Huston, David
Huston, John
Hyde, Benjamin
Hyde, James
Hyde, John
Isahower, John
Jacobs, Abraham
James, Vachall
Jamison, William
Jarrett, Phillip
Jenkins, Hugh
Jenkins, Samuel
Johnson, John
Johnson, Robert
Johnston, Francis
Johnston, John
Johnston, Joseph
Johnston, Nathaniel
Johnston, Thomas
Jones, Samuel
Josey, Frederick
Josey, John
Josie, Frederick
Josie, John
Josie, John, Jr.
Josie, William
Kaler, Lewis
Kaylor, Lewis
Kaylor, Lewis Jr.
Kearn, Conrad
Kearn, Keny
Kearn, John
Kennady, Andrew
Kennady, Jennet
Kernes, Caleb
Kern, Conrod
Kern, John
Kerns, Conrad
Kerntzer, George
Kerr, Andrew
Kerr, George
Kerr, John
Kerr, Stephen
Kerr, Wilson
Ketner, George
Kihor, Conrad
Killen, William
Kilpatrick, John
Kilpatrick, Joseph
Kincaid, Andrew
Kincaid, James
Kincaid, John
King, Richard
King, Robert
King, Thomas
Kirk, John
Klotz, Hans Leonard
Kluttz, David

Kluttz, Leonard
Klutz, Jacob
Klutz, Martin
Klutz, Windle
Knight, Michael
Knop, John
Knox, Abraham
Knox, Andrew
Knox, Benjamin
Knox, James
Knox, John
Knox, Robert
Knup, Jacob
Knup, John
Knup, William
Krider, Jacob
Krite, Michael
Krotzer, Phillip
Krowell, William
Lamb, James
Lamb, John
Lambert, Thomas
Lambeth, John
Lance, Boston
Lance, John
Lathran, Aaron
Law, William
Lemley, George
Lemley. John
Lemley, Joseph
Lence, John
Lence, Peter
Lentz, Bastian
Lentz, Davalt
Lentz, Jacob
Lentz, Peter
Leonard, Elizabeth
Leopard, Henry
Lewis, James
Lewis, Peter
Lewis, William
Lightell, Benjamin
Lin, John
Linbarrier, Nicholas
Lingle, Casper
Lingle, Francis
Lingle, Lawrence
Link, Jacob
Linn, Hugh
Linn, James
Linn, Joseph
Linn, Robert
Linster, Moses
Litaker, John
Little, Daniel
Little, John
Little, Peter
Little, Thomas
Locke, Elizabeth
Locke, Esther
Locke, Francis
Locke, George
Locke, John
Locke, John B.
Locke, M. A.
Locke, Mathew
Locke, Moses A.
Locke, Richard
Locke, Robert
Logan, John
Long, Alexander
Long, Frederick
Long, John
Long, Joseph
Louchran, Lawrence
Love, Robert
Lovewasser, Jacob
Lowery, John
Lowery, Robert
Lowery, Thomas
Lowery, William
Lowrance, Abraham
Lowrance, Alexander
Lowrance, Andrew
Lowrance, David
Lowrance, Jacob
Lowrance, John
Lowrance, John Jr.
Lowrance, William
Lowry, Charles
Lowry, James
Lowry, John
Lowry, Samuel
Luckey, John
Luckey, Samuel Jr.
Luckey, Samuel Sr.
Luckie, James
Luckie, John
Luckie, Joseph
Luckie, Mary
Luckie, Richard
Luckie, Robert
Luckie, Samuel
Luckie, William
Lyall, Margaret
Lyall, Thomas
Lyerly, Christopher
Lyerly, Peter
Mack, Thomas
Mahon, Dennis
Marlin, Elijah
Marlin, James
Marlin, Joseph
Martin. Alexander
Martin, James
Martin, Robert
Martin, Samuel
Masters, George
Mauney, E.
Mauney, Valentine
Maurer, Fred
Maurer, Rudolph
Mawra, Peter Jr.
McBride, Hugh
McBride, Robert
McBride, William
McBroom, Abel
McBroom, John
McCaughey, Archibald
McCay, Spruce
McClain, Andrew
McConnaughy, Samuel
McConnel, William
McConnell, Daniel
McConnell, John

McConnell,
Montgomery
McConnell, Samuel
McConoughey, Joseph
McCorkle, Alexander
McCorkle, Joel
McCorkle, John
McCorkle, Samuel
McCraken, James
McCraken, John
McCulloch, Henry
McCulloch, James
McCulloh, Alexander
McColloh, George
McColloh, James
McCullom, Andrew
McCullon, George
McEllwrieth, John
McElwaith, John
McElwaith, Joseph
McElwaith, Robert
McElwaith, Thomas
McFeeters, Daniel
McGee, William
McGinnis, John
McGloughlan, James
McHenry, Archibald
McHenry, Henry
McKinzie, Charles
McKnight, James
McKnight, John
McKnight, William
McLain, William
McLaughlin, James
McLaughlin, John
McLean, John
McLung, John
McManus, James
McManus, Thomas
McNeely, Adam
McNeely, Archibald
McNeely, David
McNeely, Isaac
McNeely, John
McPherson, Joseph
McPherson, Robert
McQuon, Hugh
Mendenhall, George C.
Michael, Conrad
Milford, Thomas
Miller, Benedick
Miller, Casper
Miller, Christian
Miller, Christopher
Miller, David
Miller, Frederick
Miller, George
Miller, Henry
Miller, Jacob
Miller, James
Miller, John
Miller, Martin
Miller, Michael
Miller, Peter
Miller, Samuel
Miller, Thomas
Miller, Tobias
Miller, William
Miller, Windle
Misenheimer, Daniel
Misenheimer, Peter
Mitchell, John
Moler, Valentine
Montgomery, Hugh
Montgomery,
Humphrey
Moore, Audline
Moore, John
Moose, Henry
Morehead, John M.
Morgan, John
Morgan, Nathan
Morgan, Robert
Morgan, Wiley
Morr, Michael
Morrison, Andrew
Morrison, Archibald
Morrison, David
Morrison, Robert
Morrow, Allan
Morrow, James
Mowery, Jacob
Mowery. John
Mowry, A.
Moyer, Nicholas
Moyer, Simon
Mulhollan, James
Mull, John
Nealy, James
Neasbit, John
Neely, Francis
Nesbit, David
Nesbit, John
Nesbit, William
Newnan, Anthony
Newnan, Hugh
Newnan, John
Niblock, George
Niblock, William
Nichols, Jacob
Nichols, Joshua
Nivens, James
Nivens, Robert
Nixon, James
Obercash, Franz
Orton, John
Osborne, Adlai
Otten, Richard
Overcash, Jacob
Overcash, Michael
Park, Ebenezer
Noah, Noah
Parker, Drury
Parker, Richard
Parker, Richard Jr.
Parks, Ebenezer
Parks, Hugh
Parks, Noah
Partee, Charles L
Partee, Noah
Patterson, James
Patterson.,James Jr.
Patterson, John
Patton, John
Payne, Alpheus

Pearson, Richmond
Peeler, Anthony
Peeler, Michael
Pence, Valentine
Pendry, Agnes
Pendry, James
Peniston, Anthony
Penny, Alexander
Peteet, Richard
Peterson, William
Phifer, Caleb
Phifer, Margaret
Phifer, Martin
Phifer, Paul
Phillips, Enoch
Phillips, Jessie
Phillips, John
Phillips, Reuben
Phillips, Reuben Jr.
Phillips, Thomas
Phillips, William
Phipps, Isaah
Pinchback, John
Pinkston, John
Pinkston, Meshack
Pinkston, Nelly
Pinkston, Peter
Pinkston, Turner
Pinkston, William
Pinkston, Wm. Turner
Pitman, Micajah
Pless, Henry
Pless, Joseph
Plummner, William
Poole, Henry
Porter, Edmond
Porter, James
Porter, Robert
Porter, Thomas
Poston, Benjamin
Powlas, John Adam
Randleman, John
Randleman, John Jr.
Rankin, Samuel
Reaves, James
Redwine, John
Reed, Hugh
Reed, John
Reed, John Jr.
Reed, Moses
Reed, Robert
Reeves, Samuel
Rendleman. Jacob
Rendleman, John
Rendleman, John Jr.
Rendleman, Martin
Renshaw, William
Ribelin, Isaac
Ribelin, Peter
Riblin, Martin
Rice, E. B.
Rice, Isam
Rice, Johan
Rice, Phillip
Rice, William
Richause, Henry
Rimer, Nicholas
Rinehart, Jacob
Rintleman, Christopher
Rintleman, Martin
Roan. Henry
Roan, Henry Jr.
Robbley, John
Robertson, Moses
Robinson, Benjamin
Robinson, Henry
Robison, George
Robison, Henry
Robison, Hugh
Robison, Moses
Robison, Richard
Robison, William
Rodgers, John
Rogers, Allen
Rogers, Robert
Roseman, Adam
Roseman, George
Ross, Francis
Ross, John
Ross, Joseph
Rough, Daniel
Rough, John
Rounsecal, Benjamin
Rumple, Jacob
Rusher, Jacob
Rutherford, David
Rutherford, Griffith
Rutherford, Henry
Saltz, Anthony
Sammons, Grove
Sanders, Robert
Sanderson, Joseph
Satterwhite, Horace
Savitz, George
Schiles, Henry
Schiles, Jacob
Scools, John
Scott, John
Sechler, Abraham
Setzer, John
Sewell, Greenbury
Sewell, Moses
Shafer, John
Shaffer, Richard
Shaver, Abraham
Shaver, Andrew
Shaver, Jacob
Shaver, John
Shepherd, Edward
Shields, Andrew
Shields, Joseph
Shiman, John
Shinn, Benjamin
Shireman, George
Shiver, Andrew
Shooping,John
Nicholas
Short, Peter
Shrock, Henry
Shulenburger, David
Shulenburger,
Frederick
Shuping, Jacob
Shupink, Michael
Sifford, Lewis

Simmons, Phillip
Skiles, Henry
Skiles, James
Skiles, John
Slavin, William
Sloan, Henry
Sloop, Conrad
Slough, Phillip
Smart, William
Smather, Henry
Smather, Jacob
Smether, William
Smith, Eberhart
Smith, George
Smith, James
Smith, John
Smith, Joseph
Smith, Lewis
Smith, Peter
Smith, Samuel
Smith, William
Smoot, Alexander
Smother, William
Snap, Lawrence
Steele, Andrew
Steele, James
Steele, John
Steele, Robert
Steele, Samuel
Stewart, David
Stewart, James
Stirewalt, Frederick
Stirewalt, John
Stirewalt, John Jr.
Stirewalt, Michael
Stirewalt, Peter
Stokes, Christopher
Stokes, Littlebery
Stokes, Montford
Stoner, Charles
Stoner, Michael
Stories, James
Stork, Charles
Sulfin, Jacob
Swan, Charles
Swann, John D.
Swink, John
Swink, Leonard
Swink, Michael
Tate, John
Tate, Robert
Taylor, Abslom
Thomas, John
Thompson, Alexander
Thompson, Anne
Thompson, Claus
Thompson, John
Thompson, Joseph
Thompson, Moses
Thompson, Thomas
Thompson, William
Tiel, Jacob
Todd, John
Todd, John B
Todd, John Jr.
Todd, Thomas
Trease, Jacob
Trexler, John
Trexler, Peter
Tries, Adam
Trott, Absalom
Trott, Henry,
Trott, James
Trott, John
Trott, Samuel
Trott, Sarah
Troutman, Adam
Troutman, Andrew
Troutman, Michael
Troutman, Peter
Troy, John
Troy, Matthew
Turner, William
Utzman, John
Van Pool, David
Van Pool, John
Verble, Charles
Verble, John
Verrel, John
Vickers,Thomas
Virble, Charles
Voiles, James
Waddell, Hugh
Wails, John
Walker, Henry
Walker, Robert
Wallace, Samuel
Walton, Richard
Walton, William A.
Warmington, John
Wasson, Archibald
Wasson, John
Weakley, Robert
Weakly, Robert
Weant, John
Weathrow, Awalt
Webb, Caleb
Webb, Mary
Webb, Mary A.
West, William
White, Henry
White, Joseph
Wiatt, Brantley
Wiatt, Thomas
Wiley, Benjamin
Williams, Thomas
Williamson, William
Wilson, Joseph
Wilson, Samuel
Wilson, William
Winsel, Henry
Witherow, James
Witherow, John
Withrow, John
Wolfogill, Joseph
Wood, Charles
Wood, Daniel
Woods, Andrew
Woods, David
Woods, Joseph
Woods, Matthew
Woods, Robert
Woods, Samuel
Woods, William
Woodside, Archibald

Woodson, David
Woodson, David Jr.
Wray, William
Yarbough. Edward
Yoast, Jacob
Yoss, Phillip
Yost, Jacob
Yost, Phillip
Young, John
Young, Jonathan
Young, Samuel
Zivelly, Henry

Appendix E
Signers of the Keezletown Road Petition

David Chambers, John Craig, William Craig, Robert Hook, John Stephenson, Mathew Thompson Sr, Mathew Thompson Jr, and William Williams.

Appendix F
Records of Massanutten Presbyterian Church, reproduced here in the order and fashion of the original.
From: The Session Book of Peaked Mountain Church, 1759
Alexander Miller, Minister

Baptized in 1759

Jany.	Margaret Irwin	Jean Snodon
	Nathan Huston	Susanna Berry
Feby.	Anne Harrison	Eleanor Semple
	Betty Semple	Margt. Johnston
	Hugh Brewster	John Curry
	Alexr. Wilson	Margery Thomson
March	George Malcom	William Poague
	Helen Ralston	William Woodhall

Married in 1759

Febry. 20th	John Crevens	Margaret Dyre
March 6th	Isaiah Shipman	Eliz. Hodge
March 13th	Michael Carn	Eliz. Persinger
April 3rd	John Kengere	Eliz. Sargant
April 17th	Saml. Hemphill	Mary Crevens
April 17th	Christo Huffman	Barbara Evighly
Sept. 19th	John Pharis	Elizabeth Hill
Sept. 26	Thos. Spencer	Anne Duncan
9br. 19th	John Jackson	Martha Claypool
10br. 11th	Andrew Ewen	Susanna Shannon
10br. 12th	John Hopkins	Jean Gordon

Baptized 1760

Jany.	John Magil June	John Hemphill
	Jonathan Shipman	Wm Stuart
	Henry Smith	Jas. Magil
Feby.	Walter Davies	William McClure
	Mary Crevens	Dan'l Harrison

March	Sarah Craig	Jean Ewen
April	James Brewster	Sarah Frazier
	Wm. Elliot	Sarah Guin
	Thos. Lewis	William Smith
May	Robert Grey	Mary McClure
	Jean Semple	Mary Hopkins
	David Ralson	

Married 1760

Jany. First	John Pickens	Anne Oliver
Janry. 17th	John McCay	Sarah Oliver
Janry. 24th	Saml. Briggs	Mary Logan
June 28th	Joseph Dictum	Rachel Love
July 15th	Henry Armintroute	Mary Wagonier
July 29th	Henry Henry	Mary Chesnuts
Septr. 15th	Christopher Ermintrout	Susanna Bower
8br. 21	William Glasgow	Eliz. Colley
8br. 26	Wm. Gregg	Margt. Johnston
Dec. 25	Thomas Stinson (Stephenson)	Eliz. Logan

Baptized 1761

Jany.	Joanna Berry	June	Ephraim Wilson
	John Virdon		Martin Turpine
	Jas. Virdon		Wm. Sholl
	Lydia Virdon	July	Margt. McClure
	Eliz. Ralston		Mary Irwin
Febry.	Eliz. Poague		Jean Briggs
	G--n Henderson		Mary Shannon
	Sarah Duglass		John Woodal
	Wm. Curry	Aug	Wm. Gregg
March	John Brewster		Eliz. Carlile
	Eliz. Brewster		Wm. Stuart
	Sarah Lawrence		George Stringer
April	Sarah Smith		Ruth Stringer
	Jenat Brewster		Sarah Hopkins
May	John Hopkins		Sarah Smith
	Jos. Ramsey		Abraham Pickens
	Davd. Magary		

Married 1761

March 5th	Rob t Crevens	Esther Harrison
March 31	Saml. Peterson	Martha Ledgerwood
April 16	Skidmore Monsy	Mary Scot
April 20th	Henry Long	Catrina Pence

May 26th	Saml. Semple	Hannah Copeland
Septr. First	Jas. Bell	Margt. McBride
9br. 11th	Saml. Hyrons	Christian Wilson
10br. 11th	Wm. Shannon	Catrine Thaim
10br. 24th	Thos. Peterson	Margt (Harrison?)

Baptized in 1762

Feby.	Agnes Peterson	June	Mattw. Semple
	John McClure		Anne Black
	Jean Rubertson	July	Jesse Harrison
	Eliz. McKnoughtan		
		Sept.	Gideon Harrison
	Saml. Irwin		Joseph Hyrons
March	David Magil		Gideon Harrison [2x]
	Eliz. Snodon		Wm. Ralston
	Anne Greg	Octbr.	Lusk (Tim?)
	Margt. McMullen		John Lusk
April	Benj. Semple		Mary Malcom
	Robt. M'Cay	Novbr.	Eliz. Hopkins
	Hannah Crevens		Sarah Henderson
	Eliz. Crevens		Ephraim Hopkins
May	Eliz. Ewen		Joseph Crevens

Married 1762

Jany. 7th	Matthew Black	Margt. Ponder
Jany. 9th	John Peartree	Rebeckah Lovegrove
Jany. 16th	Thomas Wilmoth	Agnes Wait
Feb. 24th	Edwd. Irwin	Eliz. Curry
Feb 25th	Robert Cunningham	Margt. Kilpatrick
March 2d	John Skidmore	Magdalene Hindoll (Kinnoll)
April 1st	David Smith	Elenor Esom
April 5th	Martin Humble	Anna Delay
April 16th	Jas. Belshaw	Esther Hook
June 24	Isaac McDonald	Jean Scot
July 28	Wm. Chesnut	Catrine Callachan
August 26	Isaiah Curry	Margt. Irwin
Octbr. 28	Hugh Dickson	Mary Londey
9br. 22	Robt. Rutherford	Mary Sevier
9br. 30	Amos Bird	Sarah Bedhill
10br. 9th	Wm. Semple	Sarah Coplin
10br. 15th	Patrick Savage	Judith McThoron
10br. 27	Leonard Propst	Catrine Capliner

Married 1763

Jany. 20th	Robert McKemmy	Sarah Cunningham
Mar 17th 1763	Adam Stinson	Rebeckah Peterson (Patterson)
March 31	Jas. Wallace	Jean Baird
May 10th	Benjn. Thos.	Susanna Lewis
May 24	Geor. Bedhill	Magdalen Birde
August 10th	Benj. Harrison	Mary McClure
August 17th	John Johnston	Mary Shelpman
	Benjn. Harrison	Mary McClure
8br. 15th	Wm. Davies	Rachel Guin
8br. 20th	John Logan	Mary McClure
9br. 8th	Robt. Davies	Sarah Morse
10br 29	George Brewster	Mary Love

Baptized 1763 *The War prevents ye compleating ye list this year.*

Jany.	Agnes Marshal	---- Green
	Arnold Custard	---- Smith
	Bridget Custard	---- Davies
Feby. at Henry Smith's		
March	John Irwin	---- Williams

Baptized 1764 *The War prevents ye compleating ye list this year.*

William Laurence	Mary Hemphill
Anne Semple	Jeremiah Crevens
John McKemmy	Jenat Brown
Wm. McMullan	

Married in 1764

Jany. 19th	Robert Caldwell	Sarah Duglass
Febry. 27th	Charles Hedrigh	Barbara Conrode
March 19th	Cornelius Boman	Susanna Painter
April 10th	John Munger	Agnes Pirke
April 26th	Kelham Price	Elizth. Null
June 26th	John Harman	Mary Van Gummundie
July 9th	Saml. Curry	Jean Irwin
Novr. 6th	Obadiah Monsey	Anne McBride

Archd. Huston to Settle ye State of Pyked Mountain Congn. which is as followeth to wit of a bond from Patrick Frazier John Davison John Stephenson & James Brewster Eight pounds twelve & two pence halfpenny

Appendix G

Augusta County Militia, 1742
Captain John Buchanan's Company
Lieutenant William Evans
Ensign Joseph Cotton
Sergeant John Mitchell

Jacob Anderson
John Anderson
James Anderson
Isaac Anderson
William Armstrong
William Buchanan
Edward Boyle
Charles Campbell
James Cooke
Robert Cotton
Richard Courser
Charles Donooho
Thomas Duchart
Robert Dunlap
Samuel Dunlap
John Dyche
James Ecken
John Edmoston
Nathaniel Evans
John Gray
Samuel Gray
James Greenlee
William Hall
Andrew Hayes
Charles Hayes
Robert Huddon
William Humphery
Joseph Kanada
William Louchrage
Mathew Lyle
Andrew Martin
John Mathews
Nathaniel McClewer
Samuel McClewer
William McCoutes
John McCrosseree
Thomas McSpedan
William Mitchell
Solomon Moffot
Alexander Moore
Andrew Moore
John Moore
William Moore
Michael O'Docherty
John Paul
John Philipmaver
William Quinn
James Robinson
William Sayers
John Stephenson
James Sunderlin
Isaac Taylor
Alexander Walker
John Walker
Joseph Walker
Samuel Walker
Thomas Williams

Appendix H

Early Settlers of Present-Day Rowan County

James Alexander	1750
William Alexander, son of James	1750
James and Mary Allison	1750
Andrew Allison, brother of James	1750
Peter Arndt	1750
Charles Burnett	1751
John Burnett	1751
Samuel Burnett	1751
William Burnett	1751
George Cowan	1750
John Cowan	1750
James Deacon	1751
Alexander Dobbin	1750
David Fullerton	1751
Archibald Hamilton	1750
Robert Harris	1751
David Houston	1751
George Henry	1751
John Lynn	1751
Robert MacPherson	1751
John Nisbet	1750
Arthur Patton	1750
Lorentz Schnepp	1750
Robert Tate	1750
Samuel Young	1751

Appendix I

Settlers of Rowan County By 1762
Irish Settlement

James Andrews
James Armstrong
Mary Armstrong
William Armstrong
William Bailey
Henry Barclay
Robert Barclay
John Beard
William Beard
James Best
John Best
John Biggs
Samuel Blythe
William Boggan
John Braly
Thomas Braly
John Bunting
Charles Burnett
Patrick Campbell
James Carson
James Cathey
Henry Chambers
Samuel Cochran
Jacob Crawford
William Crawford
Hmphry Cun'ghm
John Cunningham
William Cowan
Michael Dickson
James Dobbin
John Dobbin
James Docharty
Alexander Douglass
Thomas Douglas
Samuel Galbraith
John Gillespie
Matthew Gillespie
Thomas Gillespie
James Graham
William Grant
Robert Gray
Malcom Hamilton
Robert Hardin
James Hemphill
John Hickey
Samuel Hillis
James Hynds
Francis Johnston
Robert Johnston
John Kerr
John Kilpatrick
James King
Richard King
Robert King
John Kirkpatrick
John Knox
Dennis Lafferty
Alexnder Lawrence
John Lawrence
John Little
Thomas Little
Francis Lock
John Luckie
John Luckie, Jr
Joseph Luckie
Robert Luckie
Samuel Luckie
William Luckie
William Mackey
James Martin
Samuel Martin
Hugh Mathews
Alxndr McCorkle
David McDowell
John McElwrath
Henry McHenry
Willm McKnight
Hmphry Mntgmry
Mary Murray
William Niblock
Joshua Nichols
Alpheus Paine
James Patterson
John Patterson
James Patton
John Patton
Robert Patton
Alexander Pendry
John Poston
Hugh Reed
Robert Reed
James Porter
William Porter
Robert Rankin
Samuel Rankin
George Robinson
John Robinson
Richard Robinson
William Robinson
John Russell
Griffith Ruthrford
Henry Schiles
James Scott
John Scott
John Scott, Jr
William Sleven
John Smith
Robert Steel
David Stewart
James Stewart
James Storey
David Strain
Robert Tate
John Thompson
Joseph Thompson
John Todd
Archibald Wasson

Francis Wilson
John Wilson
John Witherspoon
Matthew Woods
Robert Woods
Samuel Woods
Samuel Young

Fourth Creek Settlement

Allen Alexnder
Adam Allison
Andrew Allison
Robert Allison
Thomas Allison
David Andrew
John Archibald
Andrew Barry
David Black
Hugh Bowman
Wllm Bowman
Robert Carson
William Carson
Robert Cavin
Samuel Cavin
Geo Davidson
Joseph Davis
Patrick Duffie
John Edwards
George Elliott
Chrpher Erwin
George Erwin
William Erwin
John Fleming
Peter Fleming
George Hall
Hugh Hall
James Hall
Thomas Hall
Samuel Harriss
David Houston
John Ireland
William Ireland
John Jack
Roger Lawson
John Leech
Richard Lewis
Walter Lindsay
George McDonald
James McIlwaine
John McKee
James Miller
James Mordah
John Mordah
Andrew Morrison
James Morrison
William Morrison
John Oliphant
James Potts
John Potts
William Read
Andrew Reed
George Reed
Robert Reed
Samuel Reed
Michael Robinson
Richard Robinson
Jmes Roseborough
Robert Simonton
William Simonton
Fergus Sloan
William Stevenson
Jacob Thomas
Samuel Thornton
Hugh Waddell
James Watt
William Watt

Davidson's Creek Settlement

Robert Adams
Andrew Allison
Samuel Allison
Catherine Barry
Francis Beatty
James Crawford
William Denny
John Dickey
Joseph Gillespie
John Gullick
David Hall
John Hall
William Hall
Patrick Hamilton
Abraham Jetton
Robert Johnston
James Lambert
Hugh Lawson
Alex McCulloch
James McCulloch
John McCulloch
John McDowell
Thmas McQuown
William McRae
Hanse McWhorter
William Morrison
Andrew Neill
James Neill
William Neill
John Parks
John Sloan
Gilbert Strayhorn
Jeremiah Streater
James Tennant
Moses White
Benjamin Winsley

Appendix J

Braddock's War - August County Militia
Bounty Claimant Suit (Coleman vs. Richardson, 1808)

Henry Bailey: Sergeant
John Baynes: Military service, no claim
Alexander Bonney: Braddock's defeat at Big Meadows
William Bronaugh: First Virginia Geo. Washington
Mordecai Buckner: Qtmster, 1755/Col. Adam Stephens
Benjamin Bullett: Ensign, First Va. Rgt/Geo. Washington
Thomas Buford: Sgt. under Braddock, Lt. under Washington
John Cole: Served at Braddock's defeat at Big Meadows
Timothy Conway: Military service
Valentine Cooper: Served at Fort Dusquesne 1758
William Cromwell: Military service
Charles Croucher: Soldier, Col. Stephens Regiment
Goodrich Crump: Military service
Mathew Doran: Military service
Wm Dangerfield: Cap 1st VA Rgt under Geo. Washington
James Dunlap: Lt/Cap. Peter Hogg, Rangers killed 1758
William Fleming: Assistant Surgeon, First Va. Regiment
Andrew Fowler: Capt Andrew Lewis' Co. at Big Meadows
John Fox: Military service, no claim filed
Henry Gains: Military service
Joseph Gatewood: First VA Rgt under Geo. Washington
Nathaniel Gist: Served w/ Washington and Cap. Chris. Gist
Peter Hogg: Captain under George Washington
John Horn: Served under Col. Mercer.
William Hughes: Subaltern, Geo. Washingon's Regulars
John Huston: Military service
Thomas Kinkead: Cap. Lewis' Co/Boquet's expedition 1764
Alexander Kinney: Military service, no claim filed
Francis Kirtley: Military service
Charles Lewis: Captain under George Washington
Thomas Lovett: First VA Regiment under Geo. Washington
William Magee: Cadet, Braddock's defeat at Big Meadows
William McAnulty: Braddock's defeat at Big Meadows
George Mercer: Cap, Va. Reg. under George Washington
John Fenton Mercer: Ensign, served w/bro George in Old Va. Reg.
Thomas Morse: Hip wound,Big Meadows under Cap. Savage
Thomas Moss: Drummer, claimed carried Braddock from battle.
Robert Murphy: Served at Braddock's defeat at Big Meadows
George Muse: Lieutenant Colonel, army
Thomas Nappe: Military service, no claim filed
John Neal: With Dunmore 1774, 13th Va. Reg. 1777

John Poo: Military service
John Posey Military service
Marshall Pratt Military service
Thomas Rutherford Military service
James Samuel First Virginia Rgt under Geo. Washington
John Savage: Military service
Charles Scott Corp. in First Va. Reg. of Geo. Washington
Jesse Scott Military service
Robert Scott Military service
Francis Self Served at Braddock's defeat at Big Meadows
John Smith Military service, no claim filed
Hugh Stephenson Military service
Robert Stuart: Military service, no claim filed
John Thompson Braddock's defeat at Big Meadows
George Turner First VA Regiment under Geo. Washington
Jacob VanBraam Military service, no claim filed
James Walker Military service
Arthur Watts Military service, no claim filed
John David Wollper: Subaltern, Col. Lewis Reg. of Regulars

Appendix K

Scots-Irish Militia from Augusta County Virginia

Jacob Aberman
John Aberman
Gardner Adkins
Archibald Alexander
Francis Alexander
James Alexander
Moses Algier
Hugh Allen
James Allen
Robert Allen
Charles Allison
Chris Amontrout
George Anderson
James Anderson
Robert Anderson
William Anderson
James Anon
Sampson Archer
John Armstrong
Robert Armstrong
George Barclay
Thomas Barrow
John Baskine
Thomas Baskine
Robert Belche
David Bell
James Bell
John Bell
Samuel Bell
William Bell
Henry Beniger
Henry Benningar
Dominick Beret
James Berlane
Christopher Bingaman
John Bingaman
Anthony Black
John Black
Matthew Black
Robert Black
William Black
William Blackwood
James Blair
John Blair
William Blair
John Bowin
William Bowin
Thomas Bowne
Robert Boyd
Thomas Boyne
Robert Brackenridge
James Bradshaw
William Bratton
James Bridgetts
Samuel Briggs
John Brown
David Bryans
James Bryans
Alexander Buchanan
Andrew Buchanan
Archibald Buchanan
James Buchanan
John Buchanan
William Buchanan
James Bunton
James Burk

James Burnside
John Burton
William Buyers
Jacob Botters
Henry Bowen
John Bowen
Moses Bowen
Reice Bowen
Thomas Bowens
James Caghey
John Cain
Andrew Campbell
Hugh Campbell
James Campbell
John Campbell
Matthew Campbell
John Cantley
George Capliner
Patrick Cargon
John Carlile
Robert Carlile
William Carothers
Henry Carr
John Carr
Richard Carr
Samuel Carr
James Cartmill
William Carvin
Thomas Cashaday
Valentine Castle
Thomas Cavon
Edward Cenney
William Christopher
John Clark
William Clark
Mathias Cleeke
Christopher Clement
Arsbel Clendinin
John Clendinin
John Clerk
Joseph Clerk
Daniel Cloud
Phelty Cogh
Hyram Coler
John Colley
James Colter
Woolrey Conrad
Darby Conway
Jeremiah Copper
Martin Cornet
John Cosby
Tetrarch Couch
James Couden
James Cowdown
Alexander Craig
Robert Craig
John Cravens
William Cravens
John Crockett
George Croford
John Crosby
James Cull
James Culton
Andrew Cunningham
Jacob Cunningham
John Cunningham
Robert Cunningham
Walter Cunningham
William Cunningham
John Cunrod
Walter Cunrod
William Currey
George Davidson
James Davidson
Benjamin Davies
James Davis
John Davis
Samuel Davis
John Davison
Robert Dew
Mathias Dice
John Dickenson
Michael Dickey
Hugh Diver
Joseph Dixton
Nathaniel Donlap
Henry Downs
Abraham Duncklebery
George Dunkle
John Dunkle
James Dunlap
James Dunlap
Adam Dunlop
James Dunlop
John Dunlop
William Dyer
Abram Earhart
Michael Earhart
John Early
Michael Eberman
William Edemston
David Edmiston
Moses Edmiston
Samuel Edmiston
Jeremiah Edwards
Frederick Eister
William Elliot
Michael Erhart
Edward Ervin
William Ervin
Daniel Evans
Nathaniel Evans
John Farrell
John Finley
Robert Finley
Christopher Finney
Andrew Fitzpatrick
William Fleming
Samuel Ford
Thomas Ford
James Fowler
Nicholas Frank
John Frazier
Michael Frees
Jonas Friend
Jacob Fudge
John Fulse
John Fulton
Thomas Galbreath
David Gallaw
David Gallaway
James Gamble
James Gatlive
James Gay
John Gay

Dennis Getty
Robert Gibson
Archibald Gilkison
Archibald Gilkson
James Gillaspey
Alexander Gillespie
James Gilmore
John Gilmore
Thomas Gilmore
George Gipson
George Goodman
Jacob Goodman
Daniel Goodwin
John Gordon
Robert Gragg
William Gragg
David Graham
Jacob Graham
John Graham
Robert Graham
David Gray
James Gray
Arthur Greer
James Grimes
Robert Grimes
Jacob Grub
David Guin
John Gum
George Gunn
Robert Gwinn
Benjamin Hagler
Jacob Hagler
John Hagler
Postine Hagler
Andrew Hall
Moses Hall
Robert Hall
Moses Hambleton
Robert Hambleton
William Hambleton
George Hamer
Alexander Hamilton
Andrew Hamilton
James Hamilton
John Hamilton
Thomas Hamilton
William Hamilton
Stephen Hanburger
Benjamin Hansley
Adam Harper
Jacob Harper
Philip Harper
Leonard Harring
Gideon Harrison
John Harrison
Nathaniel Harrison
Nicholas Havener
Andrew Hays
John Hays
Hyram Hecks
Adam Hedrick
George Hedrick
Samuel Hemphill
Daniel Henderson
James Henderson
John Henderson
Michael Henderson
Samuel Henderson
William Henderson
Robert Henry
Caleb Hermon
Leonard Herren
Thomas Hicklin
Nicholas Hoffman
William Hog
Peter Hogg
Michael Hogshead
Robert Homes
William Hook
James Hooks
William Hooks
Archibald Hopkins
John Hopkins
Jacob Hornbery
James Houston
Edward Howard
John Howell
John Hudson
Thomas Hudson
Nicholas Hufman
Philip Hufman
James Hugart
Thomas Hugart
John Hughs
Robert Hunter
Holerick Hushman
Archibald Huston
James Huston
Samuel Huston
John Hutcheson
William Jackson
Andrew Jameson
John Jameson
Joseph Jenkins
John Johnson
John Johnston
Jonathan Jones
George Jordon
Abraham Keeny
Michael Kelly
James Kenaday
William Kenaday
William Kerr
Samuel Kerre
John Kilpatrick
Jacob Kindler
George King
John King
John Kinkead
Thomas Kinkead
William Kinkead
Benjamin Kinley
Conrad Kinsel
William Kinsey
Francis Kirtley
George Kite
Valentine Kite
William Kite
Ralph Laferty
David Laird
William Lapesley
John Lawn
James Lawrence
Thomas Lawrence
Gaun Leeper

Going Leeper
Alexander Legat
John Leonard
Charles Lewis
George Lewis
William Lewis
Matthew Lindsey
Adam Little
Andrew Little
James Lockart
Andrew Lockridge
James Logan
Henry Long
Hyram Long
John Long
William Long
Peter Looney
Ephraim Love
John Low
John Lowry
Patrick Lowry
Robert Lusk
Daniel Lyle
John Lyle
Samuel Lyle
Hugh Mackclure
James Magavock
Robert Magery
John Malcolm
John Malcom
George Malcomb
John Malcomb
Michael Mallow
Michael Malow
Charles Man
George Man
Jacob Man
William Mar
George Marchel
John Massey
George Matthews
John Matthews
Joshua Matthews
Richard Matthews
Sampson Matthews
William Matthews
William Matthis
John Maxwell
John Mayers
John McAlheney
Charles McAnally
Daniel McBridge
Robert McCarney
John McCay
Alexander McClanahan
James McClong
John McClong
Patrick McCloskey
James McClung
Arthur McClure
James McClure
John McClure
Halbart McClurr
Hyram McCollom
Thomas McComb
Thomas McCome
Robert McComey
Adam McCormick
Thomas McCorne
John McCoy
John McCoy
Robert McCoy
David McCroskey
James McCutchison
Samuel McCutchison
James McDowell
Samuel McDowell
William McFarland
James McFerrin
John McFerrin
Samuel McFerrin
Hugh McGarey
Robert McGarey
William McGill
Thomas McGregor
James McHenry
William McHenry
John McKay
William McKinney
Thomas Mcklemare
Daniel McKnight
James McMahon
Alexander McMullan
Samuel McMurray
Thomas McNamar
John McNeal
Dennis McNely
John Medley
James Meeter
Edward Megary
Robert Megary
John Melcum
Joseph Melcum
Nicholas Mildebarler
Adam Miller
Jacob Miller
John Miller
Patrick Miller
Peter Miller
Robert Minice
William Minter
William Mintor
John Mitchel
Robert Mitchell
George Moffett
George Moffett
John Montgomery
James Moor
David Moore
John Moore
William Moore
George Moses
Peter Moses
George Mouse
Lawrence Murphy
Henry Murray
John Murray
Thomas Nicholas
Samuel Norwood
Poston Nosler
Nicholas Null
John Osborne
Matthew Paten
Thomas Paterson
Charles Patrick

John Patrick
James Patterson
Robert Patterson
Samuel Patterson
Audley Paul
Thomas Paxton
Larkin Pearpoint
John Peary
Jacob Pence
Henry Peninger
Gunrod Peterfish
Edwin Peterson
Jacob Peterson
John Peterson
Martin Peterson
Thomas Peterson
John Phares
Martin Phillips
Gabriel Pickins
John Plunkett
Thomas Pointer
William Polog
John Porter
Patrick Porter
Thomas Powell
William Preston
Daniel Price
Thomas Pritchard
Adam Props
Michael Props
Richard Pryar
Lofftus Pullen
William Purzins
John Putt
John Putt
William Ralston
James Ramsay
Francis Randalls
Archibald Reah
Robert Reah
William Reah
Adam Reburn
John Reburn
Eldad Reed
William Reed
John Reiger
Francis Reity
Daniel Reme
Daniel Remi
Robert Rennick
Jacob Richard
John Richard
James Risk
James Robertson
David Robinson
George Robinson
John Robinson
William Robinson
George Rogers
Matthew Rolestone
William Rolestone
Jacob Rolman
Robert Ross
William Ross
George Rowland
Jacob Runkle
Charles Rush
James Rusk
John Salley
Moses Samble
Patrick Savage
David Sayer
Alexander Sayers
Sampson Sayers
David Scott
Thomas Scott
Thomas Seirl
John Seller
Samuel Semple
Matthew Shaddin
Ludwick Shadow
Edward Shanklin
John Shanklin
Richard Shanklin
William Shannon
William Shanon
Paul Shaver
William Shaw
Paul Shever
John Shields
William Shields
John Shill
George Shillinger
Isiah Shipman
Josiah Shipman
James Simpson
Nicholas Sivers
James Skidmore
Joseph Skidmore
Abraham Smith
Charles Smith
Daniel Smith
David Smith
Francis Smith
Gasper Smith
Henry Smith
John Smith
Thomas Smith
John Snodgrass
Thomas Spence
Thomas Spencer
John Sproul
John Sprout
James Steel
Robert Steel
James Steele
James Steenson
Adam Stephenson
James Stephenson
John Stephenson
Thomas Stephenson
Alexander Steuart
David Steuart
James Steuart
Adam Stevenson
James Stevenson
John Stevenson
Robert Stevenson
James Stewart
William Stewart
John Still
John Stilt
Timothy Stoten
Cornelius Sullivan
Cornelius Sullivant

Alexander Sutherland
William Taylor
William Tencher
Alexander Thompson
John Thompson
Moses Thompson
Robert Thompson
Robert Thomson
Mathias Tice
John Tinley
James Tobit
Samuel Todd
David Tolford
Robert Tolford
Arthur Trader
Robert Tremble
John Trimble
Robert Trimble
Walter Trimble
Peter Trusler
James Turk
Gunrod Umble
Martin Umble
Ury Umble
John Vance
Thomas Vance
Peter Vanimon
Joseph Vauhob
Peter Veneman
Ludowick Wagoner
Alexander Walker
John Walker
James Ward
Joseph Ward
William Ward
James Wardlaw
John Wardlaw
George Watts
Cornelius White
Moses Whiteside
Jonathan Whitley
Jacob Wiece
Joseph Wiece
John Willey
Robert Willey
John Williams
Charles Wilson
George Wilson
Hugh Wilson
James Wilson
John Wilson
Josiah Wilson
Richard Wilson
William Wilson
John Withlaw
John Wizer
John Woods
William Woods
Richard Yedley
James Young
John Young

Appendix L

Rockingham County Virginia Militia
John Stevenson's Company

John Beck
Joseph Beckett
William Bennett
James Blackstone
Richard Blackstone
James Boswick
Daniel Bradley
Samuel Bradley
Henry Broyles
William Burns
Jesse Buzan
Thomas Clifton
Betts Collier
Patrick Collins
Leven Cooper
John Cox
Samuel Cornwell
John Crawford
William Darville
Joseph Davis
Kinsey Davis
William Davis
Henry Dawson
John Dawson
Frank Duke
Osborne Flynn
Thomas Foster
William Foster
Nathaniel Fox
Thomas Gwynn
Joseph Hall
Lawrence Harrison
Nicholas Harrison
William Holliday
William Hollis
Philip Jackson
William Jeffries
William Juks
Absolom Kent
Henry Kersey
William Kersey
John Knight
Hancock Lee
Daniel Leet
Kiah Lindsay
John Lion
James Little
William Lock
George Main
John Marks
Thomas Marks
James Mason
Forence McCarty
William McIntire
Jacob Meek
William Miller
John Minter
James Moody
Charles Morgan Jr
Samuel Murphey
John Moore
Thomas Moore
Joseph Mount
Hugh Newell
Hugh Newell Jr
William Newell
Gariot Nugent
James Parks
William Phillips
Charles Poague
Jonas Potts
George Pretty
Tom Ravenscroft
Thomas Reagan
John Reardon
Thomas Reardon
John Redman
Isaac Scissal
Linsfield Sharp
John Smith
Peter Stacy
William Stephens
Hugh Stinson
Edward Stuart
William Taylor
Philip Thompson
James Trimble
James Vaenscraft
William Vineyard
Thomas Waller
Peter Warren
Samuel Wells
James Whaley
Moses White
John White
David Williams
James Wilson
William Wilson
James Winkfield
James Wood
Robert Worthington

CPSIA information can be obtained at www.ICGtesting.com
Printed in the USA
BVOW01s2214151214

379143BV00001BA/230/P